To Yayeh

with love

[signature] Mary

07-18-2021

ASCENDING

to

HEAVEN

Ancient Churches
and Monasteries of
Ethiopia

infoAddis Publishing, LLC
202-899-0357
Alexandria, VA 22310
www.infoAddis.com
ISBN: 978-0-9856829-2-7

Created by infoAddis Publishing, LLC. A great deal of effort was exerted to limit errors and omissions. Nevertheless, the publisher cannot accept responsibility for errors, omissions, or the consequences of any reliance on the information provided.

Front cover: Monks ascending to the top of Debre Damo, a flat-topped mountain and a sixth-century monastery. Dust jacket front leaf: A photo of the three monks and description of the title. Back cover: A priest from Abune Abrham Debre Tsion Church. Dust jacket back leaf: Picture of the author taken during a visit to Abune Abraham Debre Tsion church, and blurb about him.

This book is dedicated to my mother whose interest in
my projects was equal to my own.

Tsege Gebremeskel
(1931 - 2016)

Holding on to your love.

I am forever grateful for your love. Living with me in
memory, now and forever more.

One of her proudest moments was inspecting my first book,
Ethiopia, Inspiring Journey.

CONTENTS

88

116

ACKNOWLEDGMENTS

Writing a book on the ancient churches of Ethiopia, their backgrounds and classic assertions is harder than I could have ever imagined. It took heartfelt affirmations, words of encouragement, and meaningful contributions from many people. I thank the following people for believing in my dream and helping me achieve my goal of writing this book.

First and foremost, my gratitude to scores of clergymen, for without their positive attitude and hospitality, I could not have completed this book. *Chapy Ethiopia*, for encouraging me to work on this project and accompanying me in most of the journey. Your engaging topics sparked endless conversations and made rough ways seem smoother, long distances shorter, and challenges bearable. Your knowledge of the country, appreciation of its cultures, and respect to humanity make you a perfect companion for traveling in Ethiopia. Even though you have repeatedly traveled to many of the places, you still continue to show an excitement of a first-time traveler. You are truly blessed with the quality of imprinting lasting memories. *Joseph Meaza*, when I dragged you to remote countryside, mountains, and valleys that are naturally less desirable for a child, you forgave me of my fatuity and continued to join me on my next adventure. The countless times we spent glued to the screen, watching travel documentaries, dreaming of places we want to see and adventures we want to do, are truly the times I will remember forever. I hope our experiences instilled a sense of humility and compassion to your developing views of our world. If they don't, I would still be satisfied with having a son who has done many cool things any adult would envy. *Ephrem Gino*, you have a unique personality with great passions to match it. Our travels to Erta Ale and some of the churches in Northern Ethiopia are as memorable as the places we visited. I admire your infectious lust for life and determination to correct the misunderstood stories of Africa. May your passions continue to overflow and touch many more souls. *Abush (Lalibela), Aregawi (Gerhalta), Zelalem (Bahir Dar), Haile (Axum), and Berhanu (Gondar)*, I profited immensely from your keen specialties of the respective cities. Thank you for your passion, friendship, and continued help in understanding the nuances. *Abba Hailemariam and Abba Yemane Birhan of the Waldeba Monastery*, you made my friends and me feel welcomed, comfortable, and appreciated. Your genuineness is one I only dreamed of encountering in my heavenly life. Thank you for being an important part of my story. *Abba Habtemariam and Ato Samson Agidie*, without your guidance, the trip to the Waldeba Monastery would have been complicated. Thank you for your directions and encouragements. *Alehubel Teshome*, Thank you for reviewing the content of the book. Your contribution is much appreciated.

PREFACE

This book is aimed at those who are captivated by the stories of Ethiopia and are eager to expand their knowledge to its ancient churches and monasteries. The book is also intended to spark the curiosity of historians and courageous travelers who are interested in pursuing their own firsthand experiences. I have included the profiles of over 50 churches and monasteries. Although the coverage is extensive, it is only a fraction of the many ancient churches in Ethiopia.

My work on this book is not a claim for having had a spiritual awakening nor a pilgrimage in search of healing a broken soul. However, my continuously evolving understanding of the order of the church, the monastic life of the monks, and the intricacies of the Ethiopian Orthodox Tewahedo Christian religion fed my curiosity and gave me the edge to thoroughly document and enthusiastically travel the required distances. Abba Gebremeskel, a priest in the remote monastery of Abba Giyorgis-Ze-Gasecha, ascribed my interest to publish a book about Ethiopia's ancient churches and monasteries to a calling from God. He said in a very convincing and deliberate manner,

"It is not you who chose the project. It was chosen for you by the Higher Power."

If, in fact, that is the case, I hope my work adequately portrays the extraordinary minds that created these establishments and the sincerity of the pure souls I encountered in Ethiopia's ancient churches and monasteries.

The genesis of my interest was the degree of humility I encountered all over Ethiopia. The clergy and the devout followers are a true embodiment of their faith and align spiritually to the teaching of Christ. Furthermore, they strive to imitate His values. They simply attempt to live His words to their literal meanings.

"Whoever exalts himself shall be humbled, and whoever humbles himself shall be exalted"
(Luke 14:11).

Opposite page: Merigeta Shewangizaw Melku of Lalibela, designing an illuminated manuscript that illustrate the stories from the Bible. Top: Abba Hailemariam, a monk in the Waldeba Monastery, resting after a long day of walking from Abrentate to Tsesote (two locations within the monastery).

It is refreshing to witness humility, respect, and honesty coexisting to form a near-perfect soul. Such behaviors are observed in the extraordinary work of Abba Gebremeskel, a 34-year-old monk who recently hewed four churches out of rocks in Gashena, near Lalibela. Researchers and historians shall devote much time to study the significance of his work and his contribution to strengthening the religion in years to come. Speaking with him in detail about his work makes it clear where he wants to dedicate the glory of his work. I was beyond belief on the magnitude of his accomplishments but more impressed by his ingeniousness.

Although visiting these ancient churches and monasteries would impress most visitors, one does not have to be of the faith to appreciate the brilliant minds that created the structures, the strong bond that allowed centuries of continuity, and the calm state of mind of the current guardians. The generation of caretakers sustained the environment with meaningful interactions, uplifting conversations, deep silence, and refreshing degree of humility that transport most visitors toward a state of peace and tranquility.

Even though most of the ancient churches and monasteries are found in remote sites and hard-to-reach elevations, monks and clergy continue to inhabit the structures and perform daily services. Some clergymen walk miles and climb peaks of mountains to showcase their churches to visitors, often repeatedly. For visitors like me, the serene natural setting surrounding many of the churches often enhance the allure and highlight the peaceful quality. However, it can be an exhilarating adventure to reach them as many require ascending uncomfortable heights, inching near edges of mountains and jumping over big drops.

It is misleading to mention all the glowing results without stating the challenges I encountered throughout the trip. Fortunately, the challenges were few with limited consequences. Most guardians of the churches and monasteries were eager to show me the treasures they care for and tell me their stories, while few questioned my intention and created unnecessary obstacles. Future travelers could overcome this challenge by obtaining an authorization letter from the Ethiopian Orthodox Tewahedo Church before visiting the churches. The most common on-premise challenge is finding the person with the key to the church. In most cases, priests reside in the communities in which they serve. While they work on their other duties, it is common for a visitor to wait thirty minutes to an hour or longer for access.

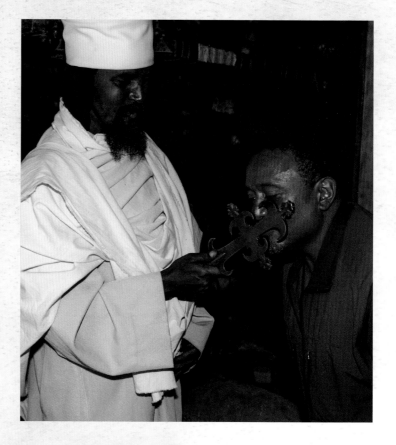

Ascending to Heaven is my third project on my native country, Ethiopia. My first book, Ethiopia: Inspiring Journey, occupies a unique place in my heart. It recounts my first trips to Ethiopia's tourism properties. It was written with a goal of introducing the readers to many of the common tourist attractions in Ethiopia. My second book, Addis Ababa: The New Flower of Africa, presents the current and historical views of the capital city, Addis Ababa. It also used Addis Ababa as a focal point and introduced the must-see places of the country.

So why did I publish this coffee-table book, my third project, about Ethiopia? Because there is more I must share with you! As simple as that!

I have included many photographs to enhance the readers' experience, strengthen their existing knowledge, and provide a prelude to those who are new to Ethiopia and are forming new bonds. Although researching the places, finding them, and taking the journey to get there are major tasks that require ample time and effort, I shall be happy to convey the pleasure and contentment I achieved from writing this book. My only regret is the exclusion of thousands of images that could have further indulged the readers.

The majority of the ancient churches and monasteries covered in this book are rock-hewn structures with limited natural light access. Candles and *twafe*, wax-based stick candles made locally, are used to further illuminate the details of the interior and the paintings adoring them. However, in few places, taking properly exposed pictures was beyond the limits of most aperture openings and shutter speed techniques. For several decades, it has been believed that the intense illumination from photographic flashes ruin delicate arts and documents; therefore,

most churches strictly enforce a no-flash policy. I augmented the camera's capabilities with less intense zoomable LED flashlight to capture as much details as possible.

As a conclusion, I contemplated on choosing words and crafting my sentences to express how I feel about my native country, Ethiopia. Luckily, I came across a paragraph that completely expresses my sentiments. Sylvia Pankhurst, in her 1955 book titled Ethiopia: A Cultural History, wrote,

Whenever I went in Ethiopia, I felt I was among friends. I derived from my visits there more happiness than I can even adequately express. All my memories of the beautiful country, its magnificent mountains and ever-changing skies, its glorious sunshine and climate of perpetual spring, its wealth of foliage and flowers, its erect and handsome people, graceful in their white national dress, are endeared to me by recollections of the constant kindness I was privileged to receive in that entrancing wonderland.

Opposite page: The author, Esubalew Meaza, receiving a blessing by kissing the ancient hand cross of Saint Yared. Top: The fresco at the very-difficult-to-get-to church, Abune Yemata Guh, in Tigray.

INTRODUCTION

Ethiopia is one of the first nations to accept Christianity. It dates to the ancient Kingdom of Axum, when King Ezana adapted the faith as the state religion in the fourth century. Those with desire to investigate the history will be met with supporting artifacts and historian views. However, the profound depth of Christianity in the Ethiopian society does not often come across as clearly to many visitors. To those following the faith, religion is the primary element of their identity. In most cases, culture is shaped by religion, as much as the practice of religion is influenced by the elements it inherited from culture.

Some accounts further elongate Ethiopia's connection to Christianity to the year AD 35. The basis to it is Acts 8:26–40, which states that an angel of the Lord instructed the apostle Phillip to help the Ethiopian eunuch, who was returning from worshipping in Jerusalem and was attempting to comprehend the book of Isaiah, understand the scripture. Upon understanding it, the Ethiopian asked to be baptized by Philip.

"Then both Philip and the eunuch went down into the water and Philip baptized him" (Acts 8:34–38).

The Ethiopians' perpetual and genuine devotion to their faith is witnessed by the timeless artifacts passed through generations. Today the Ethiopian Orthodox Tewahedo Churchs (EOTC) mark many towns, cities, and rural areas of the country. Among people who identify with the faith, life circles around religious events and shapes the world around them. It is one of the major building blocks used to generate and sustain a meaning in life. Attending one of the many colorful religious holiday celebrations underscores the profundity of the reliance.

Ethiopian Orthodox religious ceremonies are unique and impressive, especially Timket (Epiphany), Genna (Christmas), and Meskel (the finding of the true cross). Ethiopians' most ordinary mornings begin with the sounds of religious songs and chants emitting from churches. Afternoons are when clergy often home visit their flock, leading to evening, when many church grounds are used for preacher-led Bible studies. Furthermore, during festivals, clergy and followers chant, dance, and pray for a longer period.

The Ethiopian Orthodox Tewahedo Church played a critical role in the establishment of Ethiopia as a nation. The development of the alphabet, art, writings, calendar system, and language is an undisputable example. Furthermore, the creation of musical notes by Saint Yared in the early sixth century illustrates the church's direct contribution to the development of art and music. The combination of the formation of the basic system and the creation of the institutions to deliver it was accomplished by the church. In some parts of the country, the church continues to be the preferred provider of early childhood education.

Ethiopia shall soon stretch out her hands unto God.
Psalms 68:31

Opposite page: Priests dressed in ceremonial gowns and holding two types of crosses (processional and hand crosses) at the Debre Damo Monastery.

Christianity shaped Ethiopians' spiritual and intellectual life. Furthermore, music, art, and literature benefit from the church's activities. Some of the earliest writings found in Ethiopia are products of the church. Although the intention was to teach and spread religion, techniques and products developed to do so had a wider reach. For example, the art of making parchments, the ability of using plants to make dyes, and the methods of illuminating and binding manuscripts had impacting influences.

The Queen of Sheba is known as Makeda in Ethiopia. Her visit to King Solomon of Israel dates Ethiopia's awareness of the Old Testament to around 1,000 BC. According to the first book of Kings in the Old Testament, around the 10th century BC, a queen from a nation known as Sheba decided to meet the great King Solomon in person. Having heard King Solomon's wisdom, the queen brought challenging questions to test his authenticity. Having met him, the queen proclaimed that his wisdom and prosperity far surpassed the report that she had heard (1 Kings 10:7). According to Ethiopia's chronicle of royal line, the Kibre Negest, or Glory of Kings, written in the 14th century, Minilik I, who presided over the acquisition of the Ark of the Covenant, is Queen of Sheba's son by King Solomon. The acquirement of the ark marked the beginning of the imperial Solomonic Dynasty of Ethiopia.

Archeological findings attest to the earlier existence of Ethiopia. The well-known archeological findings include stone age tools and megalith, and Lucy, a hominin who lived over three million years ago. One less known relic is the oldest standing building in Ethiopia known as the Great Temple of Yeha. Dedicated to the great god of sun and moon, it is located in the town of Yeha, 54 km from the current city of Axum. Yeha was the center for an ancient kingdom called Di'amat, a kingdom composed of the local people and immigrants from Yemen. The Di'amat kingdom's South Arabian cultural influence, language, and writing system called the Sabian was then used as the backdrop to a flourishing beginning of a new kingdom called the Axum Kingdom. However, archology findings tend to reject the notion that civilization was entirely imported from South Arabia settlers. Instead, the developments in the region were on the contrary largely generated within the area itself (R. Pankhurst, 20).

Opposite page: Artist Mengestu Chernet depicts the story from the Hebrew Bible in which the Queen of Sheba visits King Solomon, the king of Israel and a son of King David. Top left: Ancient pre-Axumite frieze depicting ibex at Yeha, set on the outer wall of Enda Abba Aftse church. Bottom left: The oldest standing building in Ethiopia known as the Great Temple of Yeha. Abune Aftse, one of the Nine Saints who expanded Christianity in Ethiopia, built his monastery next to the temple. Top right: Queen of Sheba's ruin palace in Axum, Tigray.

The Kingdom of Axum is an ancient kingdom that was in the northern part of Ethiopia. The height of the kingdom is estimated to be between AD 500 and 600; however, its influence can be traced to the first seven centuries AD. The Axum civilization gained prominence through the wide range of activities, including international trade. As a center in the Roma-Indian trade route, Axum's gold, silver, and copper coinages went into circulation. As an indicator of Axum's trade activities, Ethiopia's antiquity coins were found in Arabia and as far as India. "They traded with countries as far apart as Egypt and India, as well as Arebia, and exported ivory, gold in exchange for textiles and variety of manufactured good" (Friedlander, xviii).

The city of Axum is home to many obelisks. The granite stelas, dating back to the fourth century, are believed to be burial monuments for Axum's rulers. The elaborate mausoleums underneath them underscore the belief and show the powerful and influential nature of the kingdom. The large ones located in the northern park are ornamented with two false doors at the base and multistory false windows. The stela's size indicated the prominence of the regal.

The Axumite civilization is a credited with the adaption and expansion of Christianity throughout Ethiopia. King Ezana, who ruled between AD 330 and 356, accepted Christianity as the state religion around AD 341 . "Axumite coins minted after AD 341, wherein the older sun and moon symbols are replaced by a cross" (Briggs, 20).

The introduction of Christianity to the king had an ill-fated beginning. When a ship carrying Christian merchant Meropius of Tyre made a prevision dock at a Red Sea port, a conflict arose, resulting in the killing of all but two young boys on board, Frumentius and Aedesius. The two boys were taken to Ezana's father, King Amida. Upon the death of the king, Frumentius' close relationship with the successor, King Ezana, gave him the clout to convert the heir to the throne to Christianity. The Coptic Patriarch of Alexandria, Egypt, subsequently appointed Frumentius as Ethiopia's first bishop. Ethiopians venerate Frumentius, whom they call Abba Selama (father of peace) and Serte Birhan (source of light).

One significant window to King Ezana's Axum Kingdom is the various inscriptions discovered. The most insightful is the stone found by three local farmers: Mr. Godefa Leghese, Mr. Tsegay Hagos, and Mr. Kahsay Welde-Gerima. It is inscribed using three languages (South Arabian [Sabian], Greek, and Ge'ez) and celebrates the victories of King Ezana and his army. Furthermore, inscribed coins made in gold, silver, and bronze indicate the intricate depth and advancement of the Axum Kingdom. The Axumites first began producing coins around AD 270, under the rule of King Endubis. Axum was the first African civilization, not including African cities under the Roman Empire, to produce coins (Pankhurst, 26). The coinage system also provided timeline to the conversion of King Ezana to Christianity. Pre-Christian South Arabian symbols, sun disc, and moon crest were replaced by the cross of Christ.

Opposite page: The second tallest stela, 24.6-meter-high and 170 tones in weight. Looted by Fascist Italy in 1937. It was transported to Italy in three pieces. The obelisk was then returned to Ethiopia in 2005. Top left: A mausoleum, a multichambered royal cemetery under the tallest (fallen) stela. Image shows the corridor. Bottom Left: Two images showing the Ezana Stone in its entirety and close-up, respectively.

Top right: Gobo Dura (Mount Dura). A quarry about five kilometers from the city of Axum. This is the source of the Axumite stelae and stone monuments. Unfinished stelae and markers on how the stones were cut can be seen. Bottom right: Lioness of Gobo Dura. According to locals, this rock sculpture of a lioness was carved in the 10th century to protect the town after the destruction caused by Queen Yodit.

CHURCH BUILDINGS

Most rock-hewn churches covered in this book are constructed on a hill or top of a plateau or nestled halfway on a cliff. Beside the discernable explanation of isolation, the church ascribes a biblical and symbolic interpretation to the site selection. The two biblical inspirations are God giving the Ark of the Covenant to Moses on Debre (mountain) Sinai (Exodus 34:1–9) and Jesus Christ preaching on mountains (Mark 9:2–8, Matthew 24:3) (B.Taddesse, 121).

The Ethiopian Orthodox Tewahedo Church buildings are broadly categorized into three styles: basilica, rectangular, and round. The basilica design is believed to be influenced by the Middle Eastern Orthodox churches (Salvo, 59). The rectangular-shaped churches include the ancient monolithic, semi-monolithic, cave, and built buildings supported by four walls. They are supposed to have been adopted from the Old Testament to resemble a synagogue (B.Taddesse, 123). However, the dominant church architecture for the last 600 years has been the circular type (Phillipson, 25). Regardless of the type and shape of the church, it must have three sections with a degree of holiness attribution: Qene Mahlet, Kedest, and Mekdese.

The round church buildings are divided into three concentric ambulatories. The outside ambulatory of

Right: A diagram created by Mamo Meaza, showing the circular church design and its concentric ambulatories. Opposite page: A group of Merigeta, highly educated debtera (cantors) singing and dancing using (Tsenasel) sistrum, and (meqwamia) prayer staffs. To become a Mergeta, one must go through over 15 years of education, which includes Qene, Zema, and Akwakwam.

a circular church is called Qene Mahlet (choir), the place where the debtera (cantors) sing hymns. The second chamber is known as Kedest, where liturgical processions happen and the Holy Communion is administered. The innermost and the most sacred place of the building is known as Mekdese (sanctuary). The Mekdes is usually square in shape and consists of the Menber (altar), on which the tabot, the replica of the Ark of the Covenant, is placed .

Not all the rock-hewn and rectangular churches have spaces partitioned for Qene Mahlet and Kedest. However, they have designated areas in front of the Mekdes, where the Holy Communion and hymnals are performed.

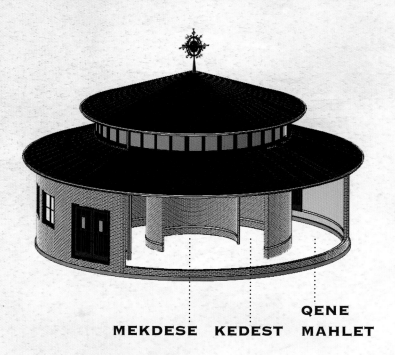

MEKDESE KEDEST QENE MAHLET

YEHA

Debre Damo ✝

ADIGRAT ●

✝ Abba Garima

ADWA ●

GHERALTA
MOUNTAINS

AXUM ●

FREWEYNI ●

HAWZEN ●

MEGAB ●

Daniel Korkor
Mariam Korkor

Abune Yemata

Abreha and Atsbeha ✝

✝ Abune Gebremikael

DEGUM ●

Abba Yohanni ✝

WEKRO ●

Mariam Papasetti ✝

Yohannes Maequddi ✝

Abune Abreham, Debre Tsion ✝

THE COMING OF CHRISTIANITY

Synaxaria and various gedles (hagiographies) credit nine monks (depicted in the painting below) for the expansion of Christianity in Ethiopia. According to Gedle Aregawi and Gedle Pentalewon, their coming to Ethiopia occurred during the reign of Ella Amida II, the sixth king after Abrha and Asbeha (Selassie, 116). The disagreement between the Oriental Orthodoxy and the rest of the churches on the issue of whether Jesus was human or divine was widely acknowledged to have been their reason for traveling to Ethiopia. In AD 415, the Council of Chalcedon's decision to affirm the deity and humanity of Christ to remain distinct drove the nine monks to search for a country where the religious practices aligned with their belief. For this reason, they were not tolerated in the Roman Empire and were obligated to leave for Ethiopia (Selassie, 116). Regardless of the reason, the Ethiopian Orthodox Tewahedo Church acknowledges their contribution in strengthening the faith, introducing monasticism, and establishing various monasteries. The church canonized the monks and remembers them with great reverence.

Yodit (Judith), a non-Christian queen who destroyed churches and monuments with the goal of eradicating members of the Axum Kingdom, rose to prominence in the 10th century. The inseparable nature of church and state made churches and monasteries in North Ethiopia as equal targets to her destruction. "The Beja, one of the people ruled by the Axumite Kingdom, represented the most difficult group to subdue for the Axum Kingdom" (Asante, 96) In fact, King Ezana of Axum once sent his own brothers, Sheazana and Hadefa, to concur the Beja. However, the Beja's defiance and consistent attacks eventually weakened the Axumites and created an environment for Yodit to overthrow the kingdom

Yodit is known in Ethiopia by two distinct names: Yodit Gudit (Evil Yodet) and Esato (the fire). The locals used these names to symbolize her vindictiveness and destructive behavior. After the death of Gudit, Anbesa Wudm came to the throne and then peace and order was restored (Selassie,228).

GHERALTA MOUNTAINS

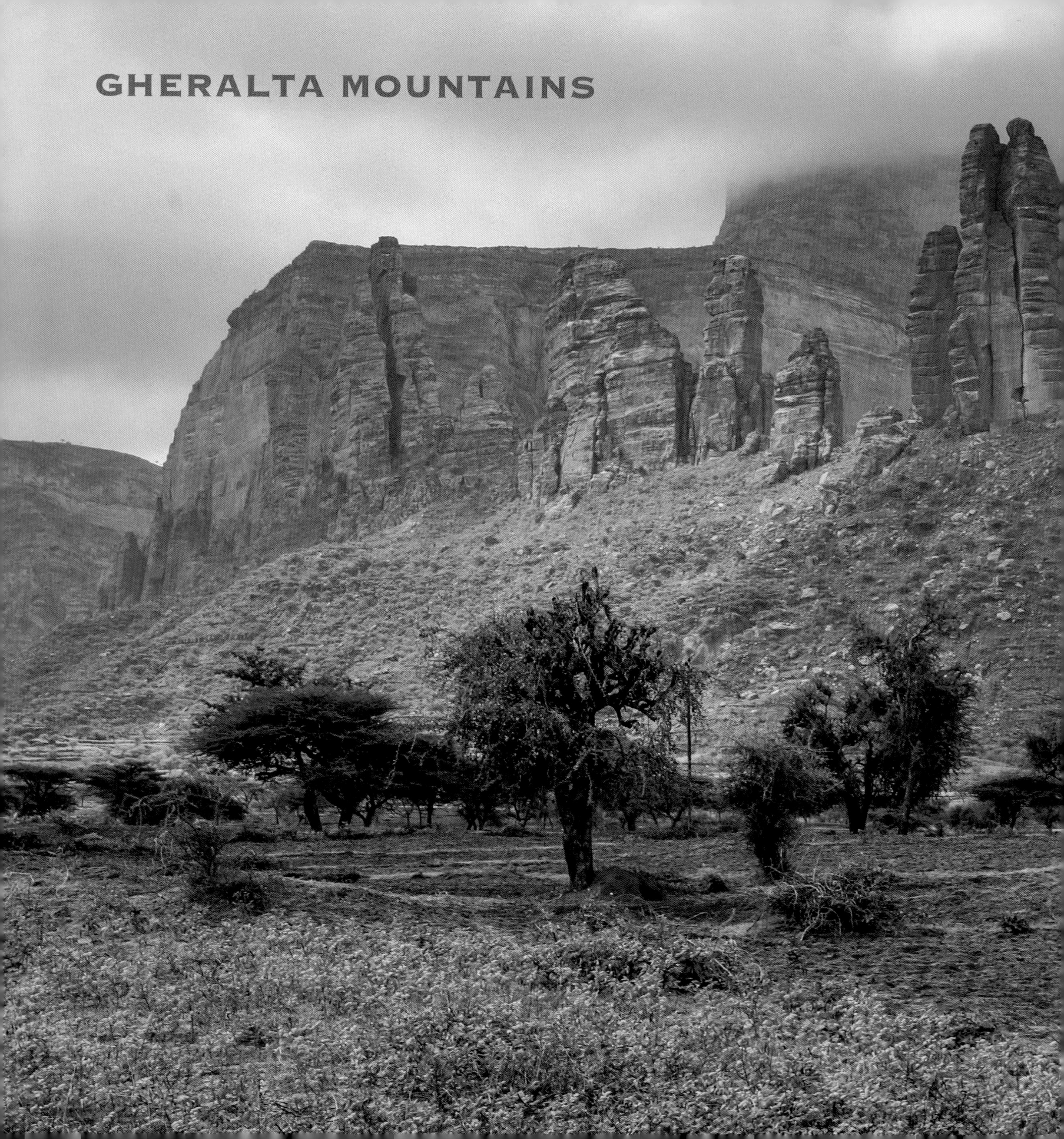

THE NINE SAINTS

Abba Aragawi – Founder of the well-known monastery of Debre Damo (cover page picture). The saint is said to have used a serpent to summit Debre (mountain) Damo, where he built a monastery. Abba Aragawi is also the founder of monastic life in Ethiopia: "He established among his children the Rules of Monastic Life, which he had learned in the house of his father Pachomius" (Budge, The Book of the Saints of the Ethiopian Church, vol. I, p. 155). His commemoration is on Tiqemt 14 Ethiopian Calendar (ET)/October 25. Abba Pentalewon – Settled in Axum, he is remembered for having helped King Kaleb by his prayers during the march crossing the Red Sea to rescue the Christian community. He is known as the Pentalewon of the cell for having never left his praying cell. This saint dwelled for many days in silence and solitude; he never laughed, and he never spoke to anyone, but he wept for his sin day and night. His monastery is located at the top of Qoho hill in Axum. His commemoration is on Tiqemt 06/October 17. Abba Garima – He founded a monastery at Madara, near Adwa, in Tigray. He is remembered on Sene 17 (ET)/June 24. Abba Aftse – He settled in a pre-Christianity Sabaean site called Yeha. His feast is celebrated on Ginbot 29 (ET)/June 6. Abba Gubba – He founded a hermitage near that of Abba Garima, west of Madara. He is remembered with Abba Aftse on Ginbot 29 (ET)/June 6. Abba Alef – He founded a monastery at Debra Halle-Luya. He is commemorated on Megabit 11 (ET)/March 20. Abba Yemata – He established his church in the Gerhalta region. His feast is on Tiqmet 28/November 8. Abba Liqanos - He is remembered twice a year. Hedar 25 (ET)/December 4/5 and Tir 4 (ET)/January 12/13. Abba Sehma settled on a plateau near Adwa. Today the area is called Enda Abba Sehma. He is remembered on Tir 16 (ET)/January 24/25. (Portella, 52-53), (Selassie, 117-118).

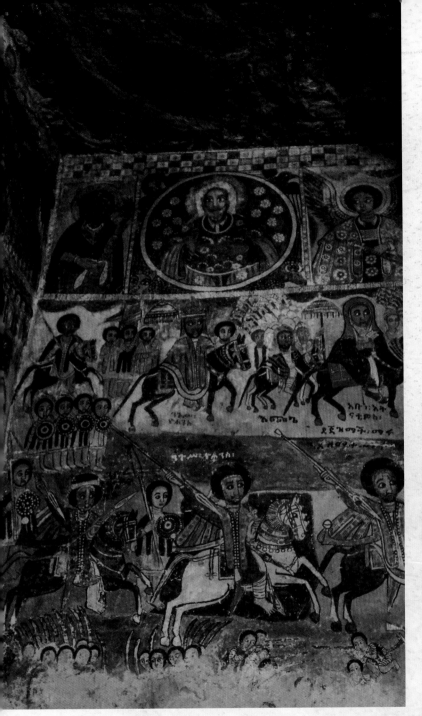

ABREHA AND ATSBEHA

Abreha and Atsbeha is one of the oldest and well-known rock-cut churches in Tigray. Unlike many inaccessible churches in the region, Abreha and Atsbeha is situated alongside a paved road, only 20 km west of the town of Wukro. According to tradition, the semi-monolithic church was constructed in the fourth century by the two royal brothers, Abreha and Atsbeha. The brothers, originally named Ezana and Sezana, adopted Christianity and became known as Abreha and Atsbeha. The church is known for its peculiar interior, intricate ceiling pattern, and stunning murals.

Opposite page: The main entrance gate to Abreha and Atsbeha. Top: A fresco showing God the Father in a mandorla between Mary and Archangel Michael. Below them are scenes of the Ethiopians going into war against the Egyptians at the Battle of Gundet. Right: The painting of the Kings Abraha and Atsbeha located inside the Patriarchate Museum and library in Addis Ababa.

According to a caretaker priest, the ceiling was partially covered in gold but was burned during the invasion of Ahmad Gragn. The ceiling shows discoloration that supports his claim.

Bottom: The grand wooden entrance door opens into murals and paintings depicting stories from the Bible. Right: A priest reading scriptures from an ancient handwritten manuscript.

WUKRO CHERKOS

Wukro Cherkos is a semi-monolithic church located near the town of Wukro, visible from the main Wukro to Adigrat road. Many people know of this church because of its proximity to town.

"The church has been compared to Abreha and Atsbeha and Mikael Imba [see page 49], since all three are cruciform in plan and with their facade freestanding" (Plant, 91)

Opposite page: The freestanding facade showing the main entrance as well as two side doors. Top: A ceiling covered with intricate patterns of crosses but showing disfiguration because of water seepage. Right: Students attending the traditional teaching of the Ethiopian Orthodox Church in Wukro Cherkos, learning religion, humility, manners, decorum that may lead to becoming deacon, priest, or active participants of the church.

Left and opposite page: A priest from Abune Yemata, dressed in a ceremonial gown, stands at the ledge of the church, holding on a processional cross on the picture to the left and a handwritten and illuminated manuscript on the opposite page. Top: Abune Yemata is located halfway up a sheer rock pinnacle. The leap of faith necessary to climb the rocks, cross narrow ledge, and jump drops with fatal consequences adds to the ascending excitement and leaves you with interesting post-climb stories. The invaluable assistance you get from the local guides include stepping strategy, continual supervision, and physical support when needed. According to the locals, there has never been a fatal accident.

ABUNE YEMATA GUH

Abune Yemata Guh is a monolithic church named after Abba Yemata of the Nine Saints who arrived in Ethiopia in the fourth century. The church is known for its difficult accessibility, dome, and wall paintings dating back to its founding days. Accessing the church requires scaling a sheer wall of rock without the protection of climbing ropes or harnesses. It also involves inching along narrow ledges and crossing a makeshift bridge. Those with nerves of steel and able to remain calm during the climb will be rewarded by a stunning view of the valley and the rising rocks of the Gheralta region.

"There's nowhere on earth quite like Abune Yemata Guh" (Lonely Planet).

Saint Abune Yemata is one of the many revered saints in Ethiopia. Many believe in his protection and risk the dangerous journey to receive blessing at his church. It is remarkable to see mothers with infant secure on their back maneuver the rocks to have them baptized there. The inside of the church is decorated with well-preserved frescoes that garnish two cupolas. The fresco on the outer dome is of nine apostles with the other three (Thomas, Peter, and Paul) on a wall nearby. On the inner copula is a painting depicting the Nine Saints who are widely credited for the rapid expansion of Christianity in Ethiopia. The view of the surrounding, the adventurous ascend, and the well-preserved paintings make Abune Yemata Ghu a must-see church of the Gheralta region.

MARIAM KORKOR

Mariam Korkor and Daniel Korkor are two churches crowning the pinnacle of one of the Gheralta mountains. Korkor is a local word that means a fracture, which explains a narrow crack in the face of the mountain one must hike to get to the churches. Getting to the churches requires a one-and-half-hour demanding hike through a canyon and courageous climb across and over boulder rocks. Mariam Korkor has an unassuming facade, an entrance to a semi-monolithic cave church, complete with arches, cruciform pillars, and ancient religious frescoes.

According to the priest at Mariam Korkor, the church was built by a local priest named Abba Daniel of Gheralta. He was inspired by Frumentius, the Syrian boy who later converted Kings Ezana and Sezana to Christianity, to build the church.

Opposite page: A built-up entrance facade to Mariam Korkor, a semi-monolithic cave church. Right: One of the cruciform pillars inside the church. Bottom: Recessed ceiling designs.

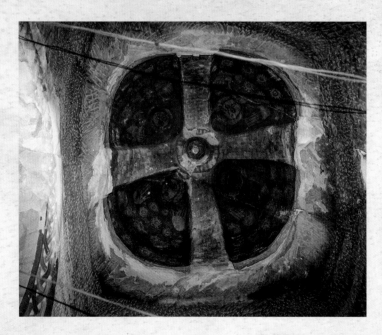

The blind arch on the north wall of the church is painted with depictions of various stories from the Bible. On the right side of the fresco is the depiction of Eve covering her nudity with a leaf and about to pick an apple while the snake is whispering in her ear. To the right of her is Adam covering in a similar manner.

DANIEL KORKOR

Daniel Korkor is located just a few minutes walk, on a dizzying ledge, from Mariam Korkor. The church is composed of two small chambers. The whitewashed ceiling and walls are sprinkled with religious paintings that are unique from other churches of its time.

"The paintings in Daniel Korkor are colourful, primitive and naive" (Frieblander, p. 104).

Left: The caretaker monk lifts the curtain revealing the entrance to the smaller chamber. Above the entrance, a painting that depicts King David playing his lyre next to Saint George on the south wall. Bottom: Saint Merkoreus on this horse. Opposite page: A painting on the ceiling depicting archangels in praying position as well as Mary and Child on her left knee.

MARIAM PAPASEIT

Mariam Papaseit is one of the most accessible churches in the Gheralta region. It is located under a mountain ledge, hidden in a green oasis. In a moderate pace, and without stopping to take photos of the picturesque landscape, one can get to the church within an hour walk. The church is a semi-monolithic structure and has its sanctuary hewn from the rock while the narthex is built against it.

Right top: Entrance to Mariam Papasette beneath an overarching cliff. Right bottom: Memorable view of Mariam Papasette, surrounded by palm trees. Bottom: A painting showing three of the Nine Saints in a praying position. Opposite page: A mural depicting Saint George rescuing a boy.

ዘ፡ከመ፡አዉ ፀዩ፡ቅዱ ፡አ ጊ ፡
ርፌ ፡ሰቢ ጋፎ ፡

Left: A mural depicting the crowning of Saint Mary as the Queen of Heaven. Top: Miracle of the Sea Monster. Archangel Rafael spearing the sea monster. Opposite page: A mural depicting the story of Adam and Eve, where Satan, disguised as a serpent, tempted Eve to sin and eat from the forbidden fruit.

ABUNE ABRAHAM DEBRE TSION

Situated at the of top of Mount Zion, the 14th-century monastic church of Debre Tsion was founded by Abune Abraham. Debre Tsion is one of the most decorated churches in the region. However, the colors are not as vivid as they once seemed to be because of old age. The architectural features include decorated cupolas and carved crosses on the walls and ceiling. One of the highlights of the church is a 15th-century ceremonial fan with wooden framework. It is one of the must-see churches in Tigray.

Top: Skillfully designed and partially damaged calling. Bottom: The 15th-century ceremonial fan is a 36-sectioned parchment book of illustrations. Paintings include of Saint Mary and Child, apostles, and saints. Opposite page: North-facing facade and the main entrance door leading into the church.

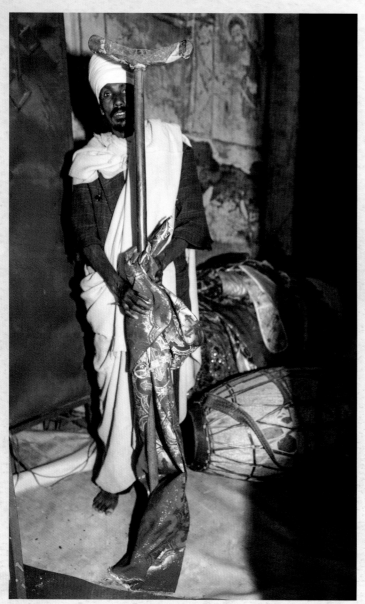

Left: Abune Abraham's personal prayer staff. A relic closely guarded by the priest. Right: The wide space surrounding the church allows clergy to circle the church comfortably. A common practice of the Ethiopian Orthodox Tewahedo religion during celebration. Opposite page: A mural depicting Abune Abraham using his cross to part the flooded Geba River so that four disciples can make their way to church.

ABUNE GEBREMIKAEL KORARO

Abune Gebremikael is one of the hidden gems of Gheralta. The vivid blue and yellow paintings covering the walls and ceiling of the church are among the best preserved in the region. The vibrant frescoes adapt into the skillfully caved columns, cruciform pillars, cupolas, and arches. Like the other churches in the area, the journey to get to it is strenuous. It requires climbing steep mountainside and uncomfortable rock hopping. Because of its distance and difficulty, many make the mistake of skipping to visit it. For those who decided to make it part of their itinerary, the church often becomes one of their favorites.

Bottom: The built-up whitewashed entrance to the church is integrated into the mountain. Right: The central dome of the church depicts the twelve Elders of the Apocalypse wearing crowns and robes as well as holding censers and hand crosses.

Top: Abune Gebremikael church's caretaker priest standing at the top of the cliff that leads to the church. Shown in the background is the picturesque landscape of the region. Opposite page: The west dome adorned by a painting of the two saints, Saint Gelawdous and Saint George, on their horses.

YOHANNES MAEQUDDI

The rock-hewn church of Yohannes Maequddi is a church dedicated to Saint John the Evangelist. It is carved out of a ridge of white sandstone mountain. One of the attractions of the church is its distinct style of painting. The style and looks of the murals covering the walls and ceiling are different from the other churches. The entire interior of the church is painted with scenes from the Bible, portraits of saints, and cleverly integrated geometric patterns. A moderate one-hour walk from the parking area is required to get to this church.

Bottom: Mural on the west wall depicting Eve tempting Adam while the serpent looks on. Below them, a Melekte Mote (messenger of death) beating a man that is hanging upside down. Right: The entrance of the church tucked into the cliff. Opposite page: A collage depicting portraits of saints, cavalry and foot soldiers, and Archangels Michael and Gabriel to the right and left of Saint Mary and Child.

PETROS AND PAULOS

Petros and Paulos is one of the smallest churches in the area. Tucked into the belly of the mountain, the wood, stone, and mortar contrast gives the church a distinctive look. The whitewashed facade, visible from the main road, initially intimidates. When first seen from distance, it is impossible to figure out the way up. However, getting to the church only requires a few minutes walk and a climb on a 15-meter makeshift ladder. Like the many churches in the Gheralta range, the interior walls are covered with paintings of various biblical characters.

Right: The view of the whitewashed facade and the makeshift ladder. Bottom: The missing cross makes this painting a unique depiction of Crucifixion. Opposite page: The entrance and built-up extension of the partly hewn wood, stone, and mortar church.

Left: A painting depicting Jesus raising Adam and Eve from hell.
Right: Saint Mary and Child on the arch leading to the sanctuary.
Archangels Michael and Gabriel left and right, respectively.
Opposite page: The picturesque landscape seen from the narrow landing area in front to the church's entrance.

MEDHANEALEM
ADI KESHO

Medhanealem Adi Kesho is one of the easily accessed churches in the area. It is five kilometers from the main road, marked by the faded signpost. The church is completely rock-hewn, with fascinating windows and door. The main entrance has distinct windows with paintings of God the Savior (Medhanealem) on the left and a cross on the right and center. A visit to this church can easily be combined with Petros and Paulos church.

"One of the truly great churches of Tigray"
(Plant, 135).

Right: One of the features of the church is a simple and creative ancient lock mechanism. The caretaker priest can demonstrate the technique inside the church. Bottom: The entrance to the church compound. Opposite page: The main view of the church, including the cemetery in front.

MIKAEL IMBA

Mikael Imba dates back to the 11th century. It is one of the largest churches in the region. It is three-quarter monolith with 25 pillars holding a six-meter-high ceiling. The church is situated in a flat-topped hill about nine kilometers south of the town of Atsbi. From the base of the hill, it requires a 15-minute ascend and climbing an old wooden ladder or the newer, more stable metal ladder.

Opposite page: Getting to the top of the Amba requires climbing a steep rock face and stepladder. Bottom: A rock-cut pool of holy water used to heal the sick. Right: Joseph Meaza opting to use the unsteady wooden stepladder to ascend to the top.

Top: The entrance to Mikael Imba. The church is dedicated to the archangel Michael. "This is one of the great churches of Tigray, and with Wukro Cherkos and Abreha-Atsbeha have been partly cut from the rock, while the rest of the Tigray churches are all hidden behind a facade" (Plant, 98).

Top: One of the resident emahoye (Holy Mother/Female Monk) in front of the lower plains.

ABBA YOHANNI

Abba Yohanni Monastery, a 14th-century rock-hewn church, is located halfway up a high cliff on the western face of a mountain called Debre Ansa in the Tembein region. The whitewashed wall, built to repair the damage to the front of the church, contrasts with the red rock background and stands out. The monastery is named after Abba Yohanni, who is believed to have excavated it. Although it seems impossible to reach at first, as you get closer to the base of the mountain, an ascending path unveils, which includes newly constructed staircases, maze of tunnels, and corners.

Opposite page: Abba Yohanni Monastery on Debre Ansa mountain seen from a distance. Right: Staircase built into the side of the rock that leads to the entrance of the monastery. Bottom: A priest reading manuscripts in front of paintings that depict St. George slaying the dragon and Mary and Child.

Top: The 12 apostles. Top 5 apostles and artist Giyorgis standing to their right. The remaining seven apostles on the second row. Opposite page left: A caretaker priest stands in front of the entrance cavity of the church. Opposite page right: Paintings on one of the pillars of the church. The painting depicts the Trinity above and a winged Abba Yonnie at the bottom.

The text on the painting reads:

ሰላም ለብ
ኣቱ ኤል
ጽ ፈን
ሃር
ንኡ

Left: Hanging rocks used as church bells. Right: A painting depicting Saint Raphael the Archangel.

Top: Clergy reading scriptures inside the tunnel that leads into the main church.

DEBRE DAMO

Debre Damo is a monastery located on a plateau about 90 km northeast of the city of Axum. The founder, Abune Aregawi, is said to have been provided with a large serpent to help him climb the 15-meter sheer cliff required to reach the top. As getting to it is arduous, parishioners and visitors are challenged to mimic his climb with the aid of a rope.

"The monastery's formidable cliffs make for one of Ethiopia's most memorable experiences"
(Lonely Planet).

It is one of Ethiopia's important monasteries. It dates back to the sixth century, during the Axum Kingdom and the reign of King Gebremeskel. It is dedicated to the founder, Abune Argawi, one of the Nine Saints, who played an important role in growing Christianity in Ethiopia.

There are about 150 monks who live in the monastery. They have no need to leave the monastery as they are self-sufficient, growing crops and caring for livestock offered to them by the surrounding communities.

Opposite page: The mountaintop monastery of Debre Damo seen from a distance. Right: Monks pulling themselves up using a plaited leather rope to the entrance gate of the monastery. Visitors are assisted by a monk at the top.

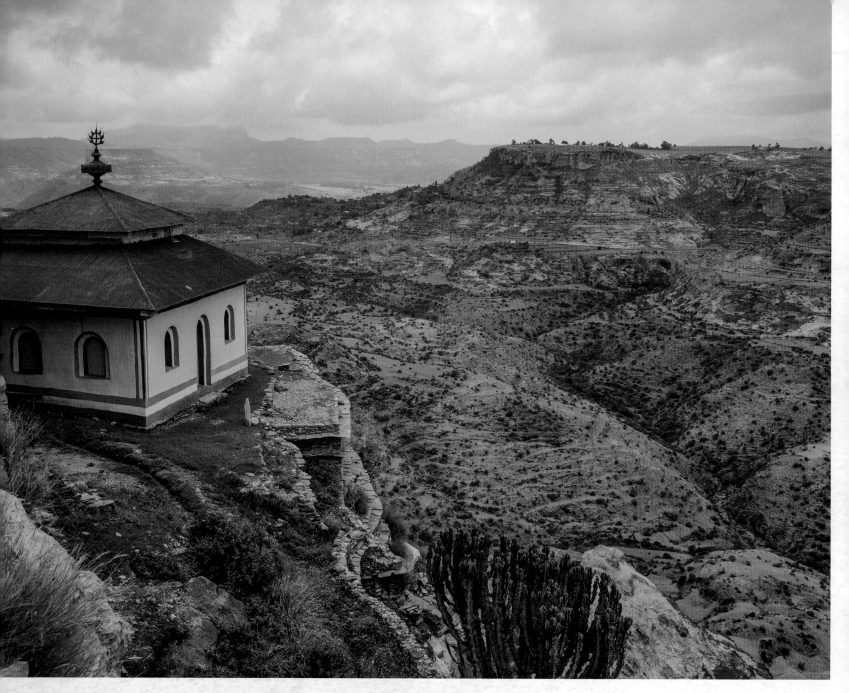

Top: Small commemorative church built at the cave where Abune Aregawi is said to have vanished. It overlooks a picturesque landscape.

Top: West facade of the main church. Bottom: Alternating courses of limestone and block of wood (monkey heads) walls are crowned with coffered ceiling. The inside of the church is adorned with hanging paintings, including two that depict the famous story of Abune Aregawi ascending to the top of Debre Damo assisted by a serpent. Right: Priests in front of the main gate to the church. They are wearing ceremonial gowns and carrying processional crosses.

Left: During the rainy season, hand-cut rock ponds are used to capture enough rainwater for an entire year. The water is covered in pondweed, which keeps it pure and drinkable. Right: Monks walking to common area from their stone houses, similar to those found in most rural communities in Tigray.

Top: Laying to rest at the monastery is an honor only few get to have. The picture above shows a body of a parishioner getting pulled up the side of the mountain for a burial service at the monastery. Those men who have the strength to make it to the top can attend the service while women say their farewells at the foothill. Only men are allowed to enter the Monastery.

PENTALEWON MONASTERY

Abba Pentalewon Monastery is located overlooking the city of Axum, on top of a tall, narrow peak. According to tradition, it was built by Abba Pentalewon, one of the Nine Saints and a man who is said to have prayed nonstop for 40 years. He is also known as Saint Abba Pentalewon of the cell, to accentuate his steady attentiveness.

Abba Pentalewon is said to have prayed for King Kalab during war against the king of Judah. The Ethiopian synaxarion (The Book of the Saints of the Ethiopian Orthodox Tewahedo Church) describes the event as,

> When Calab [Kalab] was going forth to wage war against another king, he came to Abba Pantaleon and embraced his cell, and told him his trouble. And Abba Pantaleon said, "Go in peace, for God is able to do all things, and He shall give thee victory over thy enemy"; and to return safely and in peace. When Caleb the king had come to the country of Saba, he made war on the people thereof, and he slew them all and conquered them, and there were not left any who were not scattered like leaves. And all those who saw Saint Abba Pantaleon testified concerning him, saying, "We saw Abba Pantaleon standing with us in battle, and he was overthrowing our enemies." When Caleb the king returned, having conquered the King of Judah, he forsook his kingdom, and became a monk with Abba Pantaleon (page 67).

Right: The caretaker monk showing King Kalab's tomb located on the east side of the church. Opposite page: A distant view of Pentalewon Monastery, located at the top of Qoho hill in Axum.

Opposite page: Painting of angels on the ceiling of the church's main chamber. Top: The monastery is home to many historical artifacts. Among the treasures are ancient manuscripts, a vase used by the Nine Saints, crowns of King Kalab and King Gebremeskel, and their hand crosses. Since there is no museum for the treasures, you have to settle for a friendly monk displaying them through a window.

ABBA GARIMA

Abba Garima Monastery is about seven kilometers from the city of Adwa. Saint Abba Garima is one of the Nine Saints who came to Ethiopia to expand Christianity. The monastery was established in the sixth century during the reign of King Gebremeskel. Like many of the monasteries in this region, Abba Garima Monastery is also rich with such treasures as ancient manuscripts and other artifacts. This monastery is also the final resting place for Ras Alula, an Ethiopian hero and military leader.

Left: Painting depiction of Abba Garima, one of the Nine Saints. Bottom: The mural covering the ceiling shows saints surrounded by lively geometric patterns.

ABBA AFTSE

Abba Aftse Monastery is an Ethiopian Orthodox Tewahedo Church located next to the Great Temple Yeha, a pre-Christian temple and oldest structure in sub-Saharan Africa. Abba Aftse was one of the Nine Saints credited for spreading the Orthodox faith in Ethiopia. The church was built in the 1940s over the original from the AD sixth century. The west wall incorporates a frieze ibex, a sacred animal of Southern Arabia.

Top: A frieze of six ibexes, sacred animals of ancient Southern Arabia kingdom. Bottom left: Ladies from the localities praying for the healing of the land and for a divine intervention in the form of rain. Bottom right: The steps leading to the main church.

WALDEBA MONASTERY

The word monasticism is derived from the Greek word monos, which means single or alone. Monastic living demands severe self-discipline and avoidance of all forms of indulgence, for religious reasons. According to the tradition of the Ethiopian Orthodox Tewahedo Church, the first group of monks who arrived in Ethiopia are the Nine Saints (see page 11). Monks give up worldly goods, pleasure, and despising everything, themselves included, to obey Him and love Him. They follow Christ as much as humanly possible.

Waldeba is a monastery located in North Ethiopia protected by the mighty Semen Mountain Range. It is surrounded by four rivers—Eseya, Tekeze, Zarema and Maye Weba. The remote and undisturbed setting allows the monks to pursue inner perfection and a life of solitude by removing desires and temptations.

According to Abba Kefletsadick, in his book Ye Waldeba Gedam (The Waldeba Monastery), the establishment of Waldeba is heavenly and directly connected to Jesus. In AD 485, in a town called Bulga, priests at Medhanialem Church were so immersed in the epiphany ceremonial songs and dances they neglected their responsibilities and failed to start Kedasse (mass service) on time. A hermit who informed them of their error told them that the only way to get forgiveness is to go to Jerusalem and kiss the tombs of Jesus.

The story continues to describe their journey toward Jerusalem. Unknown to them, Jesus disguised himself as a young man who volunteered to guide them. When they arrived in the present-day Sequare (part of the Waldeba landscape), He asked them, "If you see the Lord Jesus Christ here and now, would you still want to go to Jerusalem?" When they affirmed to Him that their purpose will be

fulfilled, He revealed His true identity and showed them a miracle as validation. Unsatisfied with what they saw, they continued on their journey. When they arrived at a location called *Abrentat*, He performed one more of their demand. He raised those who died during the long journey and gave strength to the weak and sick amongst them.

Seeing these miracles, they believed that He is, in fact, the Lord Jesus Christ. He then blessed the land and told them that it is their Jerusalem, and they do not have to travel to Israel. They asked the Lord to show them his crucifixion as the last rationale to truly call the land Jerusalem. Once again, he fulfilled their wish by illustrating his agony and crucifixion in front of them. This is the legendary story behind the establishment of the Waldeba Monastery. As many stories told in and around the churches, it is outside the boundaries of reason and requires a leap of faith to believe and understand. However, it is the truth as trusted by the most devoted believers of the faith.

Top left: A painting depicting Abune Samuel riding a lion. According to tradition, the Waldeba monastery was first established in the fourth century. However, Abune Samuel is known for reestablishing the monastery in the 14th century. Because of this accomplishment, he is often referred as Abba Samuel of the Wandeba. Top right: Medhanealem Church in Waldeba. Bottom: The common area used by the Waldeba monks. Opposite page: Epiphany celebration in the Waldeba monastery, near a river called Yordanos (Jordan).

QUARFE

Quarfe is a general name given to a simple type of food in the Waldeba Monastery. Although the ingredients vary slightly due to availability and season, the monastery's rule limits Quarfe to be prepared from vegetables, fruits, underground stems, and oils. The most common fruit and vegetable used are bananas and potatoes.

Preparing banana-based Quarfe takes days. Green and unripe bananas are cut and stored for a few days (usually three). They are then boiled, cooled, and peeled. A group of monks cut each peeled banana to prepare it for drying. According to Abba Fisehatsion, boiled and dried banana can be stored for a longer period and revived to freshness right before consumption. Based on availability, flaxseeds and sesame seeds are often mixed with the banana to make a meal.

Each monk has a calabash bowl he uses to transport and eat Quarfe with. Every morning the bowl is left at a designated spot near the kitchen. The teleshe* and lekabo** fill the bowl with measured portions before three o'clock in the afternoon.

*Teleshe is the person responsible for preparing and distributing Quarfe. **Lekabo is the person responsible for helping the teleshe.

Top: The teleshe and lekabo distributing Quarfe into the calabash bowls. Bottom: Sun drying potato for future use in Quarfe preparation.

Left: The Waldeba Monastery occupies a large land mass. A journey from one section to another often requires hours of varied trekking: on and around mountains, passing through valleys, and crossing rivers. Aba Hailemariam and Aba Tekelehaymanote heading to Abrentate***. Right: Aba Fisehatsion and Aba Haliemariam in a large tree locally known as Dema. It is hollowed to make a praying quarter for the monks. This extra level of seclusion offers the monks absolute silence.

*** Abrentat is the main area of the monastery.

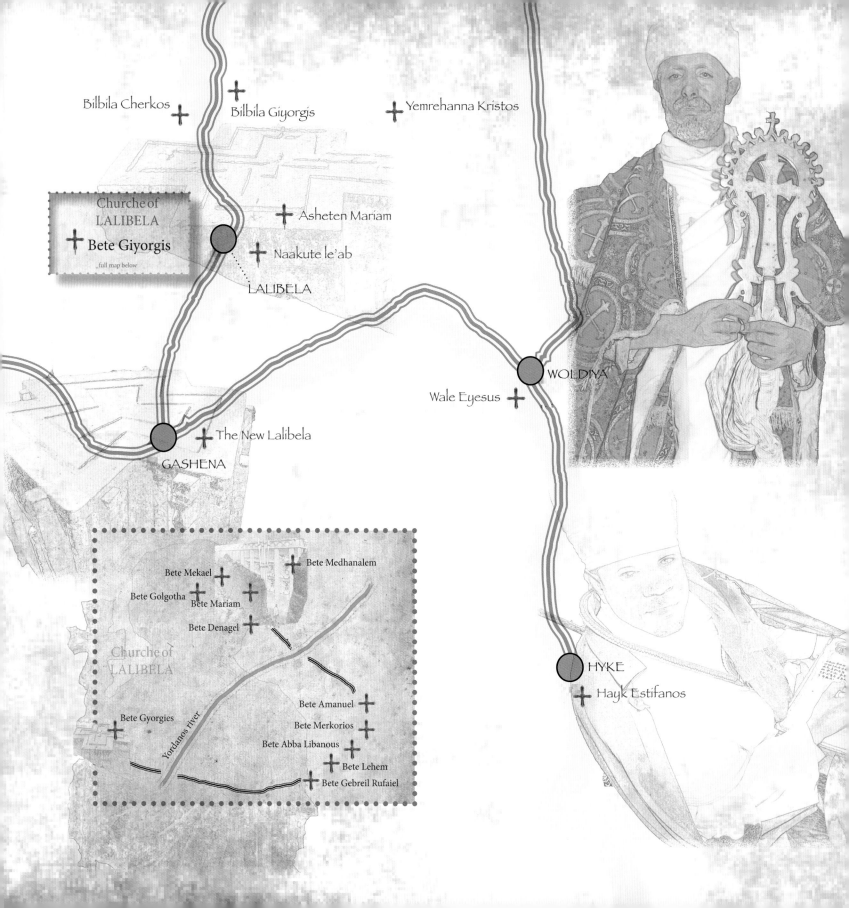

Bilbila Cherkos

Bilbila Giyorgis

Yemrehanna Kristos

Asheten Mariam

Church of
LALIBELA

Bete Giyorgis

full map below

Naakute le'ab

LALIBELA

Wale Eyesus

WOLDIYA

The New Lalibela

GASHENA

HYKE

Hayk Estifanos

Bete Medhanalem

Bete Mekael

Bete Golgotha

Bete Mariam

Bete Denagel

Church of
LALIBELA

Bete Amanuel

Bete Gyorgies

Bete Merkorios

Bete Abba Libanous

Yordanos river

Bete Lehem

Bete Gebreil Rufaiel

LALIBELA

Lalibela is a town located in the northern part of Ethiopia. The Lasta region, where the town is part of, is known for its mountainous setting and monolithic rock-hewn churches. In fact, the town is synonymous with these 12th-century living churches. The most famous of the churches ascribe their creation to King Lalibela, one of the Zagwe dynasty's king, who reigned from AD 1181 to 1221. According to tradition, King Lalibela constructed the churches as alternative site for pilgrimage to Jerusalem. During his reign, the town of Lalibela was known as Roha. Today it is one of Ethiopia's holiest places where the majority of the population is Ethiopian Orthodox Christian.

The decline of the ancient Axumite Kingdom was followed by a southward shift of the political power to Lasta and the Zagew Dynasty. Even though the dynasty inherited the Christianity faith from its predecessor, three of Zagwe's priest kings in particular are credited for the expansion by constructing churches in Lasta.

One of the priest kings, Yemrhane Krestose, built an 11th-century cave church located 42 km from Lalibela. This church is built of stone and wood, fitting to the architectural tradition of the ancient Kingdom of Axum. Priest King Lalibela is attributed with the eleven rock-hewn churches. The third is Na'akueto Le'ab, a nephew of King Lalibela, who built a cave church six kilometers east of the Lalibela churches.

According to legend, the name Lalibela was given to the king when his mother saw a swarm of bees encircling him as if they encircled their honey. As she witnessed the bees gather around her son, a spirit of prophecy revealed to her of his greatness. Thus, she named him Lalibela, the child who is graced by the bees.

Opposite page: A location map showing major towns and churches near Lalibela. Left: Priests from Saint George Church carrying *tabotes*, replicas of the Tablets of the Law

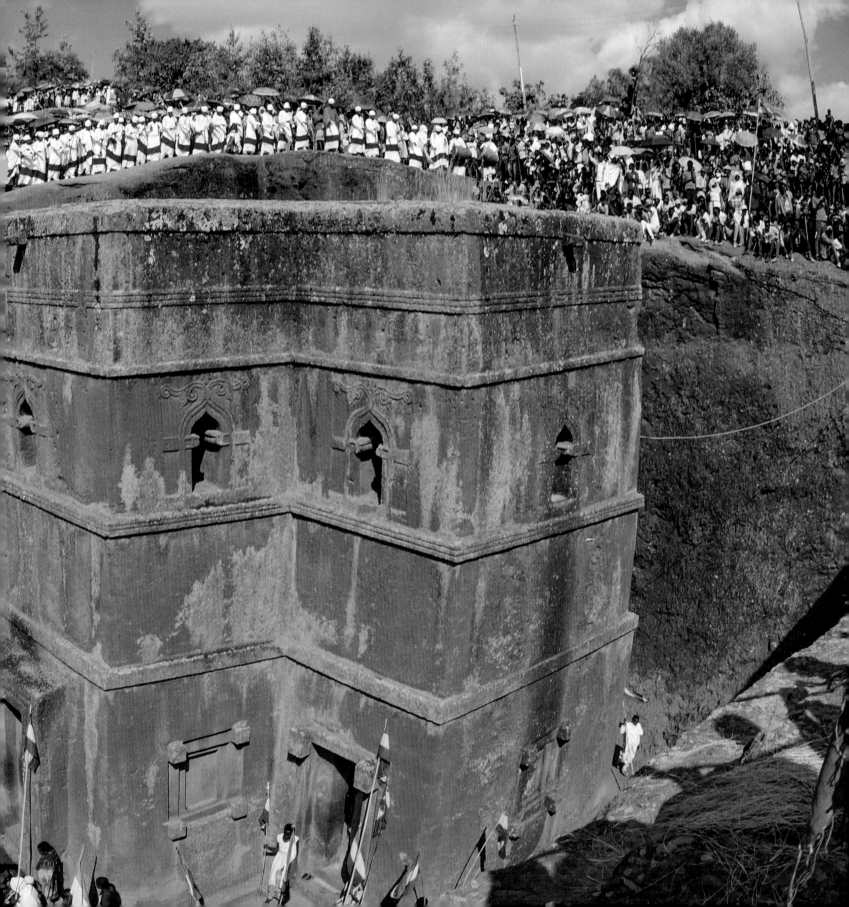

Left: A life-size relief carving on each side of the door from Golgotha to Debre Sina. Right: The rosettes on the ceiling of the south aisle at Bete Mariam adorned with geometric patterns and circular insignias.

CHURCHES OF LALIBELA

Following page: The eleven rock-hewn churches of Lalibela are situated in two groups of churches divided by a river named Yordannos (Jordan) and one isolated church. To the northwest of the river are Bete Medhanealem (House of the Savior of the World), Bete Mariam (House of Mary), Bete Meskel (House of the Cross), Bete Dengel (House of Virgin), and Bete Golgotha Mekale (House of Golgotha Mekale). The churches to the southeast of the river are Bete Amanuel (House of Emmanuel), Bete Kidus Merkorios (House of Saint Mercoreos), Bete Abba Libanos (House of Abbot Libanos), Bete Gebriel and Raphael (House of Gabriel and Raphael), and Beth Lehame (House of Holy Bread). Isolated from the two groups and located to the west is the most recognized church of all, Bete Giyorgis.

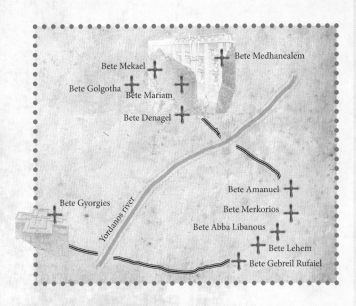

Top: The tomb of Adam decorated by a cross is a large block of stone that stands in a deep channel in front of the western face of Bete Gologota. Right: Graphical representation of the eleven rock-hewn churches of Lalibela.

ST. GEORGE DAY
CEREMONY AT
BETE GIYORGIS

AFRO AYGEBA

Afro Aygeba is a processional cross kept in Bete Medhanealem, a 12th-centruy rock-hewn church in Lalibela. The name Afro-Ayegeba roughly translates to "never returns home without victory" or "never returns home with discredit." It signifies the infallible cross and its power to perform miracles. For the Ethiopian Orthodox Tewahedo faithful, it is one of the most precious religious treasures with the power of healing the sick. The cross was stolen and smuggled out of Ethiopia in 1997 but returned to the church after few years' absence.

The design of the cross is deep-rooted in symbolism. In addition to its overall aesthetic appeal, each section signifies a biblical story. The cross image on the right has been outfitted with circular-shaped identifiers to help define the sections. The green circles represent the 12 apostles. The yellow circle in the middle symbolizes Jesus Christ during the Last Supper when He passed unleavened bread and wine and explained to His apostles that the bread represented His body and the wine His blood. The blue circles on the upper wings of the circle are reminders of the crown of thorns that was placed on the head of Jesus leading up to His crucifixion. Finally, the black circles at the lower arms of the cross represent the stick (staff) in the story of Moses parting the Red Sea. (Fanta Taddesse, Back vover).

Opposite page: A priest at Medhanealem church carrying a special cross called Afro Aygeba. Right: The Afro Aygeba cross is outfitted circular-shaped identifiers to help explain each section's meaning.

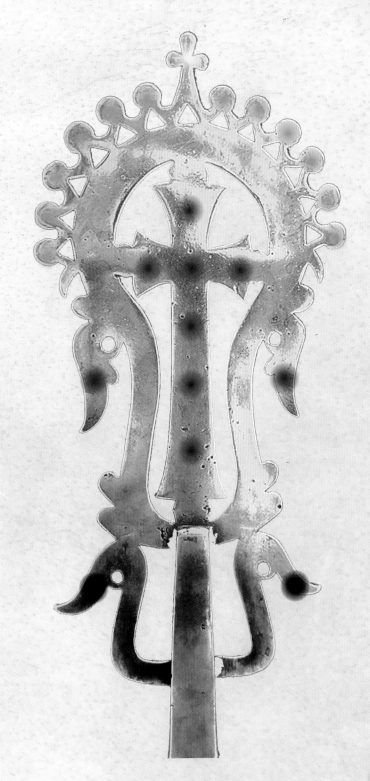

TABOT

The word tabot refers to a replica of the Tablets of the Law. It is the foundation of the Ethiopian Orthodox Tewahedo Church. Without which, a building can't be called a church. It sanctifies a church building. All churches have at least one tabot dedicated to Medhanealem (the savior of the world), Mariam (Saint Mary), Eyesus (Jesus), angels, or saints. It is kept in the Mekdese, the holy of the holiest part of the church: "The innermost area, central in a round church, at the east end in an oblong one, shut off the doors or curtains to all but priests and deacons (and in the past, to the King), is the Maqdes [Mekdese], or qeddesta qeddusan, the holy of the Holiest, where the tabot or altar tablet is kept" (Munro-Hay, p. 50).

Left: A ceremony commences during Saint George Day celebration at Bete Giyorgis. The tabot is leaving the church to spend a night at a designated place nearby. Opposite page: The Lalibela churches have many deep and slender pathways, tunnels, and bridges. The priest carrying the tabot exiting the church as clergymen with ceremonial umbrellas accompany him.

NA'AKUETO LE'AB

Na'akueto Le'ab is a cave church located on the outskirt of Lalibela, only seven kilometers from the city center. It is dedicated to King Na'akueto Le'ab, who ruled Ethiopia for 40 years during the Zagwe dynasty. He is also the nephew and successor of King Lalibela.

The church is simple and surrounded by the cave. It possesses many treasures, including some paintings, manuscripts, and crosses that belonged to King Na'akueto Le'ab. The water dripping through the crack from the natural rook roof is said to be holy. According to the priest, the water is always similar in volume, regardless of the rainy or dry season. Locals believe it to be the tears of Na'akueto Le'ab for the suffering of Jesus.

Right: An illuminated manuscript displaying Mary and Child painting. Bottom: A distant view of Na'akueto Le'ab in the rock grotto.

Left: The caretaker priest displaying a processional cross and hand cross of Na'akueto La'ab. Right: The caretaker priest uses a cup and kettle to scoop the holy water from the stone receptacles.

ASHETEN MARIAM

Situated 3,000 meters above the town of Lalibela, the Asheten Mariam Monastery is a rock-hewn church carved into a cliff face. The church's treasures include accent parchment books, detailed processional crosses, and icons. The church is accessible via a two-hour hike from Lalibela or a few minutes walking from a parking area, after a short drive using the recently built mountain road to the top of Mount Asheten.

Left: A large wooden crucifix ornamenting the inside of the church. Bottom: The last leg of the path, on Mount Asheten, leading to the entrance of the church. Opposite page: A priest holding two intricately designed processional crosses. The design of the cross on the left depicts God the Father (top), Mary and Child (left), Archangel Gabriel (center), and Saint George (right). The picture was taken in the rock tunnel leading to the church's entrance.

BILBILA GIYORGIS

Bilbila Giyorgis is a church attached to a rock and is located 30 km northwest of Lalibela. The only visible part of the church is the facade; all other parts are tucked into the rock. The highlight of the church is the bees and the hive inside the church. According to the caretaker priest, the honey from these particular bees have curative elements, especially for psychological disorders and skin issues.

Right: A priest holding a twafe, a locally made candle from honey and wax, as a light source to show the illuminated manuscript. The left side of the manuscript is illuminated with a painting of Mary and Child with Archangels Michael and Gabriel.

BILBILA CHERKOS

Bilbila Cherkos is a semi-monolithic church that dates back to the time of King Kaleb at the sixth century. The church is dedicated to Saint Cyriacus (Kirkos). According to the Ethiopian synaxarion, Saint Cyriacus (Kirkos) and Julitta (Iyalota), his mother, became martyrs, and the child, Cyriacus (Kirkos), healed many sick folks and performed great miracles.

Left: The beehive inside Bilbila Giyorgis church. Right: The caretaker priest holding a unique circular hand cross. Opposite page: The caretaker priest of Bilbila Cherkos showcasing one of the illuminated manuscripts in the church.

Top: A fresco of Moses holding a tablet of the Ten Commandments in Bilbila Cherkos.

Top: A horseman on chamber wall of Bilbila Cherkos. According to the caption below, it is Saint Kirkos.

YEMRHANE KIRSTOSE

Yemrhane Kirstose is one of the well-preserved churches in Ethiopia. It is named after a 12th century king who was also a priest and a saint. The church is located inside a natural cave, shielding it from the elements, thus contributing to its intact condition despite being in service for centuries. Visitors to the town of Lasta while visiting the more famous rock-hewn churches of Lalibela often hear about this church. However, the impressive design, the well-preserved building, a history that predates the Lalibela buildings make the 90 minutes' drive and the 20 minutes' walk through a forest of juniper trees to get to it worth it.

The exterior of the church is built with alternating wood and whitewashed stone layers, commonly known in Ethiopia as the Axumite building style. Among the attributes that make it unique in the Lasta churches is that this church was built, not excavated. It sits on wood foundations over a marshy ground. Uncovering bamboo mats unveils a hole on the cave ground, just outside the church, where visitors can see the underlying body of water. The original wooden doors and skillfully installed cruciform windows give the building its dignity and character. The doors are outfitted with functional ancient locks and ornamental brass studs.

According to the caretaker priest the tombs behind, covered with a cloth brocade, contain the remains of King Yemrhane Kirstose, his daughter, and a patriarch. The church is also known for the number of mummified bodies located deeper into the cave. These bodies are said to be of those pilgrims who came to die at this holy place.

Left: Yemrhane Kirstose church is famous for its interior decoration. A mural on the east wall depicts Jesus entering Jerusalem. Opposite page: The priest is reading from an ancient and illuminated manuscript dressed in a ceremonial gown.

Left: The intricate geometric patterns adorn medallions above the entrance. Opposite page: Elaborated and large saddleback wooden roof above the nave and the complex geometric patterns indicate expertise in craftsmanship.

THE NEW LALIBELA

There are four new rock-hewn churches built in a town called Gashena, North Wollo. A monk in his early thirties is responsible for designing and sculpting them. Skeptics have long questioned the identity of the builders of the original Lalibela churches. Some have gone the extra step by casting doubts on them being Ethiopians. Today Abba Gebremeskel and others like him are showing the world their gift for design, construction, and religious maturity for details.

Left: The intricate carved geometric patterns adorn the ceilings of the churches. Top: The triangular-shaped church is similar in appearance as Saint George. Opposite page: One of the four churches excavated by Abba Gebremeskel (standing next to it).

HAYK ESTIFANOS

Hayk Estifanos is a monastery found in North Wollo, near Lake Hayq. It is a 13th-century monastery founded by Monk Iyasu Mo'a. It is also one of the churches that got destroyed by Ahmed ibn ibrahim alQazi (a.k.a. Ahmed Gragn) in 1524. The monastery is known for producing scholars who went on to start and manage other monasteries and religious institutions in the country. Among the disciples is Saint Tekele Haymanot, who founded Debre Lebanos Monastery. Others became leaders and critical thinkers with major contributions in strengthening the faith.

The monastery houses a number of ancient artifacts, which include a parchment manuscript copy of the book of the Gospels written around 1280, a large cooking pot used by monks to cook in the 13th century, and other 13th-century objects.

WALE EYESUS

Wale Eyesus is a church located inside a cave in Weldiya, Wollo. According to the caretakes, this church was built by King Na'akueto Le'ab. Jacques Mercier and Claude Lepage, in their book Lalibela, compare masonry with the Axumite alternation of horizontal beams and masonry. This church resembles the cave church of Emakena Medhanealem located in Lasta. It takes two hours of walking in the most beautiful country landscape to get to the church.

Top: Lake Hayk is a natural tourism attraction of the monastery. It is one of the freshwater lakes in Ethiopia. It is 6.7 km long and 6 km wide and has a maximum depth of 88 meters (Museum Booklet). The monastery is surrounded by the lake and attractive birdlife. Bottom: The monks in Hayk monastery are self-sustaining, farming and growing various fruits and vegetables. The monks are removing corn kernels from the cob to prepare them for different types of food. Opposite page: Wale Eyesus, a 13th-century church built under a natural cave.

ABUNE ARON

Abune Aron is a 14th-century monastery founded by Abune Aron. It is located in a small province in North Wollo called **Mekete**. The monastery is rock-hewn and has five chambers cut in the rock. It is famous for two extraordinary roof openings. Both the ceilings of the first and main chambers are partially hollow. According to the resident priest, the cavity allows fresh air and sunlight but denies a single drop of rain to come through.

Top: The visually impaired caretaker priest, Abba Ameha Selasse, has hewn additional rooms nearby the monastery for clergy usage. Bottom: The strenuous path up to the church is a steep knifelike ridge. Most of the stretches are exposed to the elements. Therefore, walking in the midday sun makes the hike twice as difficult and tiring. Opposite page: A priest dressed in a ceremonial gown is standing under the main chamber's roof cavity, simulating the pose during all weather, thus demonstrating the phenomenal described above.

ABBA GIYORGIS ZE-GASECHA

The Abba Giyorgis ze-Gasecha Monastery is found in South Wollo, Kelela province in the town of Borena. The monastery is situated on a 96-meter high Amba (flat-topped mountain). Unlike Debre Damo, a similar monastery in Tigray, this monastery does not require a rope climb a sheer rock wall. The side of the mountain is carved, and a makeshift ladder is created using lumber.

At the top, there are various rock-hewn cavities and rooms used by the monastery. Among them is the rock-hewn church excavated by Abba Giyorgis himself. It has all three sections of the typical Ethiopian Orthodox Tewahedo Church: Qene Mahlet, Kedest, and Mekdese.

Abba Giyorgis was born in 1357 in Borena, Wollo. He is well-known for his writings, which were prolific than those of any of his predecessors. He is often compared with Saint Yared, the famous Ethiopian composer of religious music. According to his Gedel (hagiography, the writing of the life of Abba Giyorgis), he wrote over 40 books. His first book is called Arganon, which is fully dedicated to giving thanks to Saint Mary. According to legend, he communicated to Saint Mary in several occasions.

Right: A narrow path at the southwest side of the mountain is carved and outfitted with lumbers. This is the makeshift ladder used to scale the mountain leading to the entrance gate. Opposite page: A distant view of monastery, a 96-meter high Amba (flat-topped mountain).

Opposite page: The two entrances to the rock-hewn church are covered with corrugated metal roof to protect them from the elements. Left: According to his Gedel (hagiography), Abba Giyorgis is said to have the ability to directly communicate with Saint Mary. During one of her visits, she had helped him open his mind, allowing him to become a great scholar. Right: Part of a cross belonging to Abba Giyorgis is said to have healing power to this day.

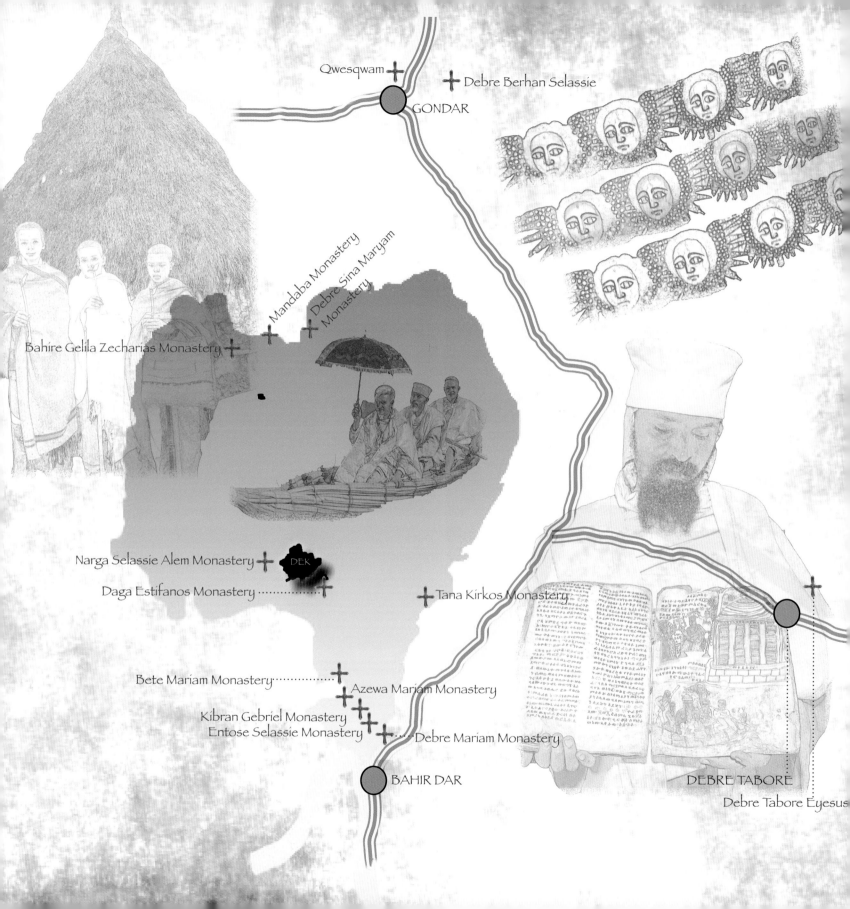

Qwesqwam ✠

✠ Debre Berhan Selassie

GONDAR

Mandaba Monastery

Debre Sina Maryam Monastery

Bahíre Gelila Zecharias Monastery ✠

Narga Selassie Alem Monastery ✠   DEK

Daga Estifanos Monastery ....

✠ Tana Kirkos Monastery

Bete Mariam Monastery ....   ✠

Azewa Mariam Monastery

Kibran Gebriel Monastery
Entose Selassie Monastery ....   Debre Mariam Monastery

BAHIR DAR

DEBRE TABORE

Debre Tabore Eyesus

LAKE TANA

Lake Tana is the largest lake in Ethiopia. It is 84 km (52 miles) long and 66 km (41 miles) wide. The maximum depth is 15 meters (49 feet). It covers 3500 Square Kilometers (1,400 square miles) and has the Blue Nile River flowing through it. The lake contains at least 37 islands, of which more than half contain Ethiopian Orthodox Tewahedo monasteries and churches. The islands are desirable locations that provide shelter and isolations for the monks.

The monasteries and churches on the islands and shores are protectors of countless ancient religious artifacts. According to tradition, Lake Tana was the hiding place for the Ark of the Covenant for over 800 years before it was returned to its original location, Axum Tsion Mariam. In most cases, the churches themselves are attractively decorated with murals and paintings that depict stories from the Bible.

The churches on the islands and the peninsulas are best accessed via boat rides. The ports at Bahir Dar and Gorgora are used to reach the churches in the south and north of the lake. Bahir Dar is a city located about 550 km north of Addis Ababa. The city is situated at the southern tip of Lake Tana. Its port is the best access point to visit the churches and monasteries in the south and middle of the lake. The churches covered in this book that use the Bahir Dar port are the Azewa Mariam Monastery, Betre Mariam Monastery, Daga Estefanos, Kibran Gebriel, Narga Selassie and Tana Kirkos, Entose Eyesus, and Abba Yohannis Monastery.

The second port is in the town of Gorgora. It is located 70 km south of the city of Gondar, at the norther end of the lake. The port is the ideal access point for visiting the churches and islands in the northern part of the lake. The churches covered in this book that use the Gorgora port are the Mandaba Monastery, Bahire Gelila Zecharias Monastery, and Debre Sina Church.

BETRE MARIAM MONASTERY

Betre Mariam is a 14th-century monastery founded by Abune Betremariam. It is located on the Zegie Peninsula near the southern shore of Lake Tana. It is a one-hour boat ride from Bahir Dar, past the islands of Entons and Kebran, followed by a 10-minute walk through small coffee plants and other vegetations. The simple facade of the church is no match to the elaborate interior paintings. According to the caretaker priest, the paintings were done in the 18th century by Aleka Engeda.

Opposite page: Betre Mariam Monastery is a round wooden church with thatched roof crowned by a cross and customary ostrich eggs. Left: Mural telling the stories of the Bible, including the story of Jesus entering into Jerusalem, and Saint Mary and Child. Right: The outer circle of the interior of the church. Following page: The wall painted with biblical characters and ceiling beams adorned with paintings of angels.

NARGA SELASSIE

The Narga Selassie Monastery is located on the western shores of Dek Island, the largest island of Lake Tana. The motorboat ride to the island takes about three hours. The monastery was established in the mid-18th century by Empress Mentewab, the wife of Atse (king) Bekafa. It is a classic round architecture. The inside of Narga Selassie is fully decorated with vivid-colored paintings of scenes from the Bible. Among the stories told is the exile of Saint Mary and her miracles.

Opposite page: The church in Narga Silassie Monastery is shaped in the classic round architecture. The oversize triforate arch doors are a work of art. Top: Large sycamore trees with long aerial roots descending to the lake surrounding the port of entry to the church. Right: The painting depicts Saint Mary and Child and Empress Mentewab at their feet.

DAGA ESTIFANOS MONASTERY

Daga Estifanos is a monastery located on Daga Island. The island is situated southeast of the much larger Dek Island. It was founded on the 13th century by Abune Hirute-Amlak. Unlike the other churches in the islands, the shape of Daga Estifanose is rectangular. According to the caretaker priest, the long rectangular shape represents Noah's Ark from the book of Genesis.

The monastery contains many ancient illuminated manuscripts, royal crowns, and artifacts. It is also the home for the mummified remains of the Ethiopian medieval period emperors: Emperor Dawit I, Zere Yakob, Susneyos, and Fasiledes.

Opposite page: The rectangular Daga Estifanose church. Bottom: The remains of Emperor Fasiledes (1632—1667). Top: Distant view the island where the monastery is located.

Opposite page: In Daga Estifanos, food is distributed through a simple but effective arrangement. Each monk brings his calabash bowl and places it under one of the signs on the wall near the kitchen. During the afternoon prayer, kitchen-designated monks place the desired type and portion to each monk's eating bowl. Around three o'clock in the afternoon, the monks take their daily allowance in their rooms and eat when they choose. For more on monastic food preparation, see Waldeba (page 70). Left and Right: Artifacts in Daga Estifanos museum include crowns of emperors, ancient illuminated manuscripts, and paintings.

TANA KIRKOS MONASTERY

Tana Kirkos is one of the oldest monasteries in Ethiopia. It is located in the eastern part of Lake Tana. The motorboat ride to Tana Kirkos takes about three and half hours. The monastery houses many religious artifacts and is home to a rich monastic life. According to tradition, the Ark of the Covenant was once kept in this monastery for 800 years. It was then moved to its current location, Axum, during King Ezana's reign. The monastery is also connected to pre-Christianity time through several archaic stone altars, fashioned in the manner of Jewish sacrificial stone altars.

When mentioning the monastery, the story of Saint Yared, the founder of Ethiopian church melody, is a must. His hand cross and the first book of melody he wrote, Digua, are kept in the museum at this monastery.

Right: One of the many ancient illuminated manuscripts kept in Tana Kirkos monastery museum. Opposite page: According to the caretaker monk, the folding wood panel book is 1,700 years old. It is a folder in the shape of a fan.

AZEWA MARIAM MONASTERY

Azwa Mariam is a small monastery located on Zege Island. The monastery is known for its wall paintings and murals. The church is surrounded by water. Traveling to the neighboring monasteries and churches are often made in a tankwa, a canoe-shaped reed boat made from papyrus.

Opposite page: The exterior of Azwa Mariam is constructed using reed walls, thatched, and is crowned by a cross and seven ostrich eggs. Bottom: The caretaker monk displaying one of the monastery's treasures, an ancient illuminated manuscript. Right: A monk at the Azwa Mariam Monastery using the power of holy water to purify the soul and release pain and anxiety or sickness. Following page: Clergy of the church traveling on Lake Tana, journey often made to other monasteries.

KIBRAN GEBRIEL MONASTERY

The Kibran Gebriel Monastery was founded by Abune Ze-Yohannes in the early 14th century. It is located on Kebran Island, a few kilometers from Bahir Dar. According to legend, Abune Za Yohannes was ordained as a monk in Debre Libanos, a monastery near Addis Ababa, by Abune Ezqeyas, a successor of Tekele Haymanot (founded a major monastery in his native province of Shewa). He is credited for killing the python local people worship using a cross as depicted on the painting below.

Opposite page left: A one-meter wooden cross with the crucifixion on one side and life of Christ, including birth and baptism, on the other. Opposite page right: A painting depicting Abune Ze-Yohannes killing the python locals used to worship. Top: A hand cross inscribed with Saint Mary and Child as well as saints. Top: An illuminated manuscript, one of the many treasures keept in the monastery. A decorated canon table (a system to indicate passages of the Gospels) painted on the left-hand page. Bottom: Kibran Gebriel, a circular building built in lime mortar and blocks of red stone.

ENTOS EYESUS MONASTERY

The Entos Eyesus Monastery is located on a small island next to Kibran Gebriel Monastery. One major difference between the two monastery is that unlike Kebran, females are allowed to enter Entos Eyesus. According to tradition, Entos Eyesus was also established by the same monk who founded Kibran Gebriel, Abune Ze Yohannes.

Right and opposite page: According to tradition, the island is named after Abba Entos, a monk who came to live in Lake Tana islands in the 15th century. A new building was built in 1990 to replace the ruined Entos Eyesus Church. The church is covered with vivid painting depicting scenes from the Bible, angels, and saints. Bottom: The small island of Entos seen next to its much bigger neighbor, Kibran island.

DEBRE MARIAM MONASTERY

The Debre Mariam Monastery is founded by Abune Tadios. This church's proximity to the city of Bahir Dar makes it one of the most visited. It is only a 20-minute boat ride or a couple of hours walking. The monastery is rich in ancient artifacts, which include illuminated manuscripts, wooden hand-painted icons, and hand and processional crosses.

Opposite page left: Hand-painted icon on wood depicts Saint Mary and Child. Opposite page top: Illuminated manuscript from the monastery's museum. Opposite page bottom: Debre Mariam, a circular building with corrugated iron roof crowned by a cross. The corrugated iron was placed on the top of the original thatch root as protection. Top: The caretake monk is showcasing ancient artifacts from the church's museum collection.

MANDABA MEDHANEALEM MONASTERY

Mandaba Medhanealem Monastery is located about five kilometers from the town of Gorgora. It takes 30 minutes by boat or 90 minutes by tankwa (a canoe-shaped papyrus reed raft). It was founded by Abune Yasay, the son of Emperor Amde Tsion. He was said to have floated on Lake Tana sitting on a stone. The stone he used to navigate the lake is now on display at the monastery. As a result of this miraculous journey, the people named the monastery Man-Ende-Abba (in short, Mandaba). The rough translation is "no one else can make this happen but Abba." It is one of the few churches with collections of ancient manuscripts, paintings, royal crowns, processional and hand crosses, and many other royal and religious artifacts. The monks in this monastery are believed to be devout and spiritually mature.

Bottom: The stone Abune Yasay used to sail on Lake Tana. Right: The caretaker monk displaying one of the ancient biblical manuscripts. Opposite page: One of the devout monks offering visitors the staple food of the monastery, special bread called dabe and (wet) stew.

DEBRE SINA MARIAM

The Debre Sina Mariam is a monastery situated on a promontory at the town of Gorgora, about one-and-a-half-hour drive from the city of Gondar. The church was founded by Abune Thomas during the reign of King Amda Tsion (1314–1344). The church walls and ceiling are covered with mural fresco paintings of scenes from the Bible, angels, and saints. As with most ancient arts, the murals show fading colors from reacting to the elements.

BAHIRE GELILA ZECHARIAS

The Bahire Gelila Zecharias Monastery is found on an island a few kilometers from the Mandaba Medhanialem. It was founded in the fourteenth centuries by Abba Zacharias. This monastery is not as maintained as the others on the islands. The Red Maltese cross at the front gives the church a distinct appraise.

Opposite page bottom: Painting of Ethiopian saints, including the Nine Saints who came to Ethiopia in the fourth century. Top: The circular church at the monastery looked after by a devout monk. Right: Distant view of Bahire Gelila, Sea of Galilee.

SAINT YARED

Saint Yared was an inventor and a legendary Ethiopian church musician. According to tradition, he was born on April 25, 505, in the city of Axum. His father, Adam, a descendant of the Axumite priesthood, tried to have Yared follow in his footsteps. However, Yared struggled and had difficulties in his early childhood education.

After repeated failure and tribulation, he witnessed an event that changed his life. Seating under a tree, he noticed a caterpillar struggling to climb a tree. Despite repeatedly failing, the caterpillar kept on repeating the process until it finally got to the leaves.

The event gave Yared the perspective he needed to maintain focus in his studies.

His persistence, prayer, and newfound resilience were rewarded by God with a gift of insight and intelligence. According to the synaxarion, Saint Yared went on to create a Zema (chant), inspired and guided by the Holy Spirit. Yared compiled the collection of chants in a book called Digua. His composition (Zema) is classified in three melodies: Ge'ez Zema, loud and strong in kind; Ezil Zema, sung in gentle voice; and Araray Zema, sorrowful and plaintive.

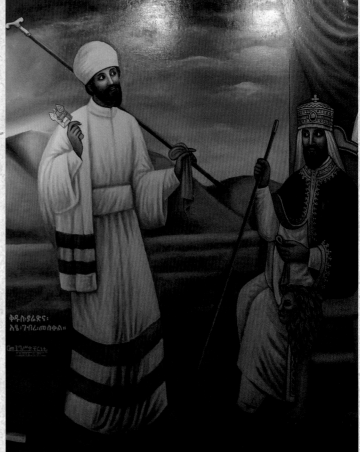

Opposite page left: Saint Yared used the two stone altars with cups carved on top to mix natural earth pigments to create black and red paints to write the first Digua, located in Tana Kirkos. In total, he created five volumes of chants for major church-related festivals: Book of Digua and Tsome Digua, chants for major church holidays and Sunday; Tsome Digua, chants for the major lent session; Book of Meraf, chants of Sabat, important holidays; Book of Zimare, chants performed after offerings and Mass; Book of Mewasit, chants for the dead. (Bekerie, 2007) Opposite page right: A painting from the Patriarchate Museum in Addis Ababa depicts Saint Yared singing in front of King Gebremeskel. The king was so captivated by Saint Yared's sweet voice and performance he accidentally spear-dug into his foot. Left: The caretaker monk displaying Saint Yared's first melody book, Digua. Right: Artifacts at Tana Kirkos include Saint Yared's hand cross.

TRADITIONAL SCHOOL

The origin of the Ethiopian Orthodox Tewahedo Church traditional schools (also known as Abenet School) is the establishment of the church. They serve both believers and the communities as a whole. Children are offered a spiritual dimension and taught the basics to help them understand the principles and literatures of the church. Furthermore, some students are encouraged to acquire advance skills to prepare them for priesthood or other callings.

The time required to complete the courses of the traditional schools depends on the level of education one receives. A typical clergyman is expected to have a common knowledge spanning in all specializations. However, to become debtera*, merigeta, kegne geta, or gera gerta, one must specialize in advanced topics. According to the Ethiopian Orthodox Tewahedo Church history, over 35 years of study is required to complete all sections of the curriculum. Furthermore, additional years of studies and practice are essential to master and specialize each section.

The study is often divided into three stages: elementary, secondary, and higher education. Nebab Bet (school of reading) is the first stage where primary education is provided. At this level, students are introduced to Fidel, the Amharic/Geez alphabet, and acquire reading and writing skills. Subsequently, they move to Kedasse Bet (the school of Liturgy), in which the Liturgy encompasses skills of praying during Mass services. Since Kedasse is the fundamental service performed in every church, competent teachers of this subject are found in abundance. Apprenticeship is another method students use to advance and master the art.

The more advanced levels include Qene Bet, Zema Bet, Aquaquam Bet and Metsehaf Bet.

Qene Bet (poetry school) is a study of literacy system and a poetic form with double-layered meanings. Students at this stage are required to philosophize and present their own expressions with Sem (wax - the apparent meaning on the surface) and underlying truth with Werq (gold). They are often challenged to react and improvise at a moment's notice.

Sem-ena-Work (wax and gold) Metaphor: Literally, wax is a natural secretion of gold that is produced in the process of purification. It is an element that covers the gold; in order to get the purest gold, it has to undergo the process of melting in fire (Mohammed, 2000).

Zema Bet (school of hymen) - In the school of zema, one may occasionally find younger pupils properly belonging to the school of reading who are taught sometimes by the master of the school or zema himself.

Aquaquam Bet (school of standing/swaying) - The body movements and ways of swaying are skills acquired through guidance. The school of aquaquam is where one receives such a training. It is a higher and more complex stage of musical training where staff (praying stick) drum and sistrums are used.

Metsehaf Bet (school of books). At this stage, students are exposed to the tradition of the church, theology, and Kenona (laws). Students are considered postgraduate and required to understand and interpret books of the Old Testament, New Testament, meshafte liqawent, and meshafe-menekosate (Tsegaye, 12)

Opposite page: Ye Kolo Temari children at Qusquam Church in Gondar. They are in front of their hut, studying the Bible. Top: Students in Debre Tabor practicing Qene, an advanced level in the traditional school curriculum. Bottom left: Ye Kolo Temari youngman armed with his stick and pouch is praying before leaving to beg for his daily food. Bottom right: Ye Kolo Temari children in Wukro Cherkos.

YE KOLO TEMARI

Ye Kolo Temari is a label given to students from the traditional teaching of the Ethiopian Orthodox Tewahedo Church. In most cases, the students travel long distances, away for their families, to attend the schools. Their main goal is to complete their education and return to serve their community as a deacon or priest (Kidane Mariam, 14). They live in small huts built by the church or by the students themselves. Their focus is education; thus, fulfilling necessities is a realistic and daily challenge. Even though some students come from capable families, they are obligated to beg for their everyday food. When asked why he begs, a student in a traditional school in Debre Tabor said, "I have to beg, I am a student of the church, and I have no other way of feeding myself."

The yeneta (lead teacher) at the church explains the multifaceted nature of begging. Children beg to feed themselves but also to learn humbleness because God hates excessive pride. They also give the community a chance to show their commitments for their religion. As they give to these students, they receive blessings for their gifts.

DEBRE BERHAN SELASSIE

Debre Berhan Selassie is a 17th-century church located in Gondar. It was built after the original church, founded by Emperor Iyasu in 1690, was destroyed by lightning. "There are said to be 44 churches in Gondar, at least seven of which date from Fasiledes' rule, but most of the original buildings were destroyed in 1888 when Gondar was attacked by the Dervish or Mahdis of Sudan." (Briggs, p. 231) According to legend, a swarm of bees had kept the invading army from burning it down.

The stone walls, arched doors, and multi-tiered thatch roofs give the church a distinct and modest look. The most striking features of the church are the glorious frescos and the mural covering the inner sanctuary. The paintings depict scenes from the Bible, angels, and saints. The ceiling is adorned with paintings of 135 big-eyed and winged-headed angels, representing the omnipresence of God. Some have been destroyed by seeping water.

Opposite page: A view of the east wall of the sanctuary. The mural of the Trinity above the wonderful rendition of the Crucifixion. Top: The exterior of the Debre Birhan Selassie Church. The rectangular stone walls, arched doors, and multi-tiered thatch roofs give the church a distinct look.

Top: Abune Melketsedek Monastery is built under a natural cave. It requires hiking down 836 steps to get to the enterance shown above. Opposite page: Bodies resisting the decay of the grave are exhumed and displayed. According to the caretaker priest, these corpses are as old as 200 years.

ABUNE MELKETSEDEK MONASTERY

The Abune Melketsedek Monastery is located in North Shewa, two kilometers from the town of Mida. The church was established in the 16th century by Abune Melketsedek. According to tradition, the monastery was destroyed by Ahmad ibn Ibrahim al-Ghazi (Gragn Mohammed), a Somali imam and general of the Adal Sultanate who fought against Ethiopian emperors. The monastery is built under a natural cave, which requires a descent of 836 steps from the main gate to the building. According to tradition, God had made a promise to Abune Melketsedek that the body of anyone buried in this monastery wouldn't decay. This legend is supported by the existence of corpses of parishioners from many years ago.

GRATITUDE

Metasebia Demessie, Professor Getachew Haile, Mamo Meaza, Emahoy Hannah Mariam, Selome-Lily Negash, Desalegn Mekonnen, Alula Kebede, Fukare Yimtatu, Aleme Tadesse, Senayet Meaza, Yemeru Tadesse, Tshaye Meaza, Kassahun Negash, Aster Zaoude, Senedu Meaza, Abiel Meaza, Sara Tesso, Hoddiyeh Dagi, Kalkidan Addis, Yemi Aberra, Yeabsira Mehari, Artist Solomon Hailu, Matt Andrea.

Your advice was invaluable, thank you.

This book was inspected by Lekawnte Gubae, a body of the Ethiopian Orthodox Tewahedo Church responsible for examining all publlished documents. My deepest gratitude for those members who participated in examining the content; and a special appreciation to Abba Habtemariam, who made the presentation on my behalf.

Opposite page: The ceiling of Debre Birhan Selassie is adorned with paintings of 135 big-eyed and winged-headed angels, representing the omnipresence of God.

FURTHER RESOURCES

A guide book to Tigrai Tourist Attractions. Discover Tigray-the Open Air Museum, Tigrai National Regional State Culture and Tourism Agency.

Aba Giyorgis Ze-Gascha. *Greetings of Angels (in Amharic)*. Megabe), 2008.

Alexis Portella, Mario. *Ethiopian And Eritrean Monasticism: The Spiritual and Cultural Heritage of Two Nations.* BP Editing, CA, 2015.

Batistoni, Milena. A Comprehensive Guide to the Rock Hew Churches of TIGRAY. Arad Books, 2015.

Batistoni, Milena. *A Guide to Lalibela*. Arad Books, 2012.

Bekerie, Ayele, *St. Yared - the great Ethiopian Composer*, http://www.tadias.com/11/29/2007/st-yared-the-great-ethiopian-composer, 2007.

Bidder, Irmgard. *Lalibela*. DuMont Schauberg, Cologne, 1958.

Briggs, Philip. *Bradt Ethiopia (Bradt Travel Guide)*, Eighth Edition. 2019.

Budge, Sir E. A. Wallis. *Kebra Nagast (English translation).* Ethiopian Series, Cambridge, Ontario, 2000.

Buxton, David. *Travels in Ethiopia.* Ernest Benn Limited, London 1949.

Chiari, Gian Paolo. *A Comprehensive Guide to Gondar and Lake Tana*. Arada Books, 2015.

Di Salvo, Mario. *Churches of Ethiopia: The Monastery of Narga Sellase*. Skira, October 1999.

Discover Amhara – *Amhara, the Home of Natural and Historic Wonders*. August 2011.

Fitzgerald, Mary Anne and Marsden, Philip. *The Living Churches of an Ancient Kingdom.* American University in Cairo Press, 2017.

Friedlander, Maria-Jose and Friedlander, Bob. *Hidden Treasures of Ethiopia: A Guide to the Remote Churches of an Ancient Land*. Shama, 2007.

Girma, Mohammed. *Whose Meaning? The Wax and Gold Tradition as a Philosophical Foundation for an Ethiopian Hermeneutic.* https://www.researchgate.net/publication/225943238_Whose_Meaning_The_Wax_and_Gold_Tradition_as_a_Philosophical_Foundation_for_an_Ethiopian_Hermeneutic, 2010.

Gobezie, Mengistu. *Lalibela: A Museum of Living Rocks*. January 2012.

Gozalbez, Javier and Cebrian, Dulce. *Touching Ethiopia.* Shama Books, 2002.

Graham, John. Exploring Ethiopia. Shama Books, 2001.

Hable-Selassie, Sergew. *Ancient and Medieval Ethiopian History to 1270*. Addis Ababa, 1972.

Meaza, Esubalew. Addis Ababa, the new flower of Africa, infoAddis publishin, 2015.

Melaku, Lulu. *History of the Ethiopian Orthodox Tewahedo Church, Parts Two and Three. From the Reign of Emperor Caleb to the End of Zagwe Dynasty and from the Classical Golder Age to the Present*. 2010.

Merahi, Kefyalew. *The Contribution of the Orthodox Tewahedo Church to the Ethiopian Civilization*. Addis Ababa, 1999.

Merahi, Kefyalew. The Meaning of Quine: the river of life. Addis Ababa, 2006.

Merahi, Kefyalew. *Peace and Reconciliation*. Addis Ababa, 2003.

Mercier, Jacques and Lepage, Claude. *Lalibela Wonder of Ethiopia, the Monolithic Churches and Their Treasures*. Shama Books, 2012.

Murphy, Dervla. *In Ethiopia With A Mule*. John Murray Pubs Ltd, 2003. 1968.

Munro-Hey, Stuart. Ethiopia, *the Unknown Land: A Cultural and Historical Guide*. I.B. Tauris Publishers, London, 2002.

Pankhurst, Richard. *The Ethiopians: A History*. 1998/2001.

Pankhurst, Sylvia. *Ethiopia A Cultural History*. Fletcher and Son Ltd, Norwich, and Leighton-Straker Bookbinding Co., London, 1955/1959.

Phillipson, David. W. *Ancient Churches of Ethiopia*. Yale University Press, New Haven and London, 2009.

Plant, Ruth. Architecture of the Tigre, Ethiopia. Ravens Educational and Development Service. 1985.

Rampone, Oscar. A souvenir Book On A Journey in Ethiopia. Commercial Bank of Ethiopia,1973.

Rasmusson, Joel. Welcome to Ethiopia. Artistic Printing Ltd. Addis Ababa, Ethiopia. 1961. Mariyn, Heldman with Munro-Hay, Struart. African Zion, the sacred art of Ethiopia. Yale University Press, New Haven and London. 1993.

Stranger, Tves-Marie, Ethiopia. Through Writers' eyes. Eland Publishing, 2016

Taddese, Haddis Rodase. *The History of the Ethiopian Orthodox Tewahedo Church (in Amharic)*, 2000.

Tadesse, Bantalem. *A Guide to the Intangible Treasures of Ethiopian Orthodox Tewahedo Church*, 2010.

Tsegaye, Mezmur. *Traditional Education of the Ethiopian OrthodoxChurch and Its Potential for Tourism Development(1975-present), https://www.academia.edu/2446790/Traditional_Education_of_the_Ethiopian_Orthodox_Church_and_Its_Potential_for_Tourism_Development_1975-present, Addis Ababa University, 2011.*

Zewde, Bahru. A history of Modern Ethiopia 1855 – 1991, second edition. Addis Ababa University Press, 2001.